FISHER BOY

Did He Catch a Big Fish Or a Girl?

Dene Weideman

B & D Press, Missouri, USA

To Dick & Joan Pisone
Bud's + my friends.
God Bless you.
Dene Weideman

ISBN-13: 978-0-615-18586-6

Published by B & D Press, Union, Missouri, USA
Cover design and image rendering by DigitalIllusionInc.com
Interior design and layout by Esther Allison

Printed in the United States of America

To Bud...

I dedicate this book to the memory of
Warren Lee (Bud) Weideman
"Twinkling Blue Eyes"
Love of My Life
Father, Grandfather, and Great-Grandfather

I wrote this book after a request from Bud a few days before
he left for Heaven. He said he had a story in mind.

"It will be about Fisher Boy."
"Did he catch the biggest fish, or was it a girl?"

Acknowledgements

I want to thank everyone who has contributed to this book, based on the life of Bud Weideman.

Consultants concerning the fishing years: Fred Allison and Ralph and Louise Maddox

Editors: Esther Allison, Joan Weideman, and Debra and Heather Weideman

Photo Imaging: Bob Weideman

Advisor: Virgil Weideman

Anecdotes: Roger and Diana Goodman and John and Sarah Goodman; Heather and Carla Weideman; Rockey and Nancy Newman and Shawn, Aaron, Brian and Amy Newman, and Sara Ebrecht and Linda Haug

Contents

CHAPTER 1

Circus Days

The last day of Pocatello, Idaho's Ringling Brother's Circus will be Saturday, September 14, 1925. John Weideman will be very busy preparing transportation cages for animals, and instructing young men to help load equipment onto the trucks that is not being used in the last acts of the circus.

John, muscular and tanned, is very strong for his 23 years, with a commanding attitude as seen in his face, with clear blue eyes and short brown hair. But in the back of his mind, worries for his expectant wife and their baby make John want to keep Nancy from helping with the work. She is always by his side, helping with whatever needs to be done.

"Nancy," John says, "You need to rest. These young squirts can handle it now. Go on to the bunk house."

A brief kiss on her cheek perks her up as she leaves, very tired and worried. After all, she is almost 29 and just having her first child. Morning Star, one of the Navaho squaws, keeps an eye on Nancy, knowing that she wants Morning Star to be a mid-wife when Nancy's baby is born.

Early Saturday morning in their cabin near Lava Hot Springs, Nancy awakes in pain and, pushing her long curly brown hair out of her face, she sits up calling John, who is snoring beside her.

"John, John, go get Morning Star. The baby is going to be here soon."

"Uh, what?" John mumbles. "It's only September 14th. What are you talking about?"

"I mean it, John. The baby is dropping, and coming very soon. Hurry, get Morning Star."

"Oh, wow!" John exclaims as he pulls on his clothes. He hurries out the door, looking back at Nancy and almost falling over the baby basket prepared for the little tyke.

"How are ya doin' honey?" asks Morning Star as she arrives. "John, fetch me some hot water and towels, then skedaddle," Morning Star says as she turns her attention to helping Nancy.

John starts his work at the circus early, getting things done quickly, and trying to look in on Nancy occasionally. A soft wailing cry comes from the cabin at 5:45 a.m., just as John is sprinting to the door to check on things.

"That's not a very strong cry for a new-born, is it?" he asks. "What do we have here, honey?" he addresses Nancy, kissing her.

"Baby boy, John. He's got your deep blue eyes and my curly hair - blond baby curls!" As Morning Star puts the crying baby into John's arms, he feels tears roll down his cheeks. The baby has a beautiful face, but his arms and legs look rather "fragile", he thinks.

Morning Star has to go see about her three little kids, one still a papoose, usually carried on her back. Her husband, Chief Brave Hunter is not too happy when the little ones awake him early in the morning.

John sits on the edge of the bed, holding the baby. "What's a good name for him, Nan?" he asks.

"What about naming him Julius after your father?" she asks.

"No, I like Warren after President Warren G. Harding. Your parents would have been proud to know we named him after the President. They liked President Harding. Too bad both of your parents are gone. Warren will never know them. They would also have been pleased to know about an Indian delivering him, since you are one-fourth Cherokee Indian."

"That's sweet thinking. We can call him Warren, Warren Lee. I like that! Thanks. He's a wonderful birthday present; born on my 29th birthday."

Warren is sleeping, and John lays him beside Nancy, smiling his big handsome smile.

"Happy Birthday, Nan." he says as he kisses her.

Before the circus pulls out to winter down south, some of the trapeze artists come by to see baby Warren. The clown also comes and brings a teddy bear to add to the rattles, tiny booties, and gowns brought by the trapeze friends.

"Where will you work now?" the clown asks.

"I will go hunting with Chief Brave Hunter until cold weather comes," John answers. "Then the baby should be well enough to travel up to Boise to visit my mother and brother. I can help my brother in the printing business."

As days go by, Nancy nurses Warren, but it seems that he isn't gaining weight like he should. He doesn't grasp their fingers when they hold a hand up to him. It worries Nancy and John, because polio is a much talked-about disease. They think maybe Warren has polio.

Morning Star comes by often and offers to help care for Warren. She takes Warren out into the sunshine. She uses some special medicinal herbs to make a paste, which she rubs on Warren's little arms and legs. His lungs still don't seem to be as strong as they should be.

Day by day, Nancy and Morning Star work with Warren, but he still doesn't improve much. Departing for Boise is postponed, since it is pretty warm near Lava Hot Springs.

Finally, by the first of December, Warren seems to be gaining weight and getting a stronger cry. However, Morning Star decides to gradually move his legs and arms a little several times a day after rubbing the salve on them. Warren seems to have pain at first, but each day it is a little easier.

Taking Warren to see grandma has to wait. Warren is getting the much needed strength in his arms and legs. When the circus comes back to the western circuit in the spring, John goes with them from city to city, letting Nancy and Morning Star continue working with Warren. They feel certain that his polio will soon be cured. Warren needs to be pulling himself up and trying out his legs, bouncing to music, etc., as babies usually do.

Warren is weaned, and Nancy begins giving him goat's milk from their pet goat, Bucky. The goat's milk is very healthful for him.

Life goes on, until Warren is three years old. His arms are strong now, allowing him to pull himself up, play with toys, and throw and catch balls. Warren hugs his teddy bear, Cuddles, while singing "Rock-a-bye Baby," swaying back and forth. Cuddles becomes his constant companion.

Early in September, 1928, Nancy thinks that for his third birthday Warren needs a birthday party.

John says, "We can invite Morning Star and Chief Brave Hunter and their children."

By late afternoon on September 14, Moonbeam, age four, and her five and six year old brothers, White Feather and Watonka, come with Morning Star and Chief Brave Hunter to visit in the Weidemans' cabin. They speak broken English.

"Welcome to our home, Chief," announces John, slightly bowing. "You and your family have been good medicine for little Warren Lee, and that has given us many smiles along the way. We say, 'Thank You', and hope you keep us in your hearts when we go west to Boise."

Chief Brave Hunter speaks, saying "We have some gifts for your little man who has taken our hearts."

Morning Star goes to Warren, sitting on his mother's lap, and puts a white leather jacket on him, helping him put his arms into it. Warren hugs her and lets her kiss Cuddles. Then Watonka brings Warren white leather moccasins and helps Nancy put them on Warren's feet.

Chief Brave Hunter takes Moonbeam and White Feather out the screen door, and unties a year-old black and white spotted dog.

The children lead the dog inside to Warren. Warren squeals with delight as he slides down from Nancy's lap and takes *his very first steps*, heading straight to the dog and hugging his neck.

Moonbeam tells Warren, "His name is Rags."

John begins singing "Happy Birthday," and everyone joins in singing and clapping. Warren is so excited he bounces along to the music! What a grand, happy occasion! All their efforts toward getting Warren well show progress at last!!

The guests sit on a long bench beside the table and John lifts Warren onto his lap, while Nancy brings the chocolate cake with chocolate icing over to the table. Everyone enjoys eating the cake.

Then John speaks, with tears in his voice. "We thank you for your very nice birthday gifts. We also have some gifts for you. Here is a picture of Warren, which we took with this box camera. We want you to have it. Also, we want to take two pictures of your family so you can have one and we can have one. A friend in the circus taught me the magic to use to make the pictures. We are very grateful to Morning Star for working with Warren so much and for your patience while she was here. We will always remember you as our friends."

The children play with Rags awhile, letting Warren hold Cuddles on Rags' back as he walks beside Rags.

When the company leaves, Nancy takes Warren to the wash stand and washes his chocolate face and hands. Then she puts an old rug down in a corner for Rags to sleep on and tucks Warren into his snug pallet.

CHAPTER 2

Life in Boise

When spring arrives, John buys a used car from one of the circus workers.

But instead of going with the circus this year, John packs up his family, their clothes, bedding and a few other items, leaving furniture in the rented house. The family travels to Boise, taking Rags with them.

When they arrive in Boise, they discover that John's mother, Leopoleina Weideman, and John's brother, Alfred, live together.

When John and Alfred's parents divorced, Leopoleina took Alfred, and Julius, their father, took John. Alfred works for William Sauer in Sauer's Printing Company. John's mother and brother are happy to have John and his family come to visit.

Julius now lives in Kansas City, and works as a carpenter. John knows from letters that his father has re-married since John left, but he has not met Minerva, Julius' new wife.

William Sauer asks John to work for him, saying they could help him and his family find a house nearby to rent. This is a welcome offer John can not turn down.

John and Nancy rent a house in Boise that has a gas cooking stove and a fire place for heating the house. They continue to use kerosene lamps for light. They have a cistern pump just outside the back door for their water, heating water in a tea kettle or pan when needed. There is a bed and a day-bed in the house, plus 4 chairs, kitchen table, and a stand-alone kitchen cupboard that has a flour bin with a sifter at the bottom.

Nancy likes the house, and John does, too, but he really does not like working all day inside a printing establishment. However, he does get paid every week and he does the work alright, helping with the printing machines.   It just is too confining. He likes to work outside.

Warren enjoys the fenced-in yard where he and Rags begin to run races and play ball. Nancy watches him joyfully from the kitchen window as she works. She plays with him in the yard much of the time, and begins calling him her "Little Buddy."

Summer flies by quickly, but by September John is homesick for Kansas City and wants to introduce Warren to his father, Julius Weideman. There is a problem, however. What should they do with Rags?

Nancy says, "It will be a sad thing for Buddy if he has to leave his racing friend. He is really running well when he plays with Rags. His little legs are getting quite strong."

On Buddy's fourth birthday there is not a party, but Grandma Weideman makes a birthday cake. After dinner and the cake, John takes Buddy and Nancy for a ride in their car. They *just happen* to stop beside a brightly-lit drugstore.

"Can we go inside?" asks Buddy.

"Oh, yes, I guess we can go inside and see what they have in there." Daddy says. "Maybe you will see something you would like to have for your birthday."

Right near the door is a soda fountain, and on the other side near the front door is a case with candy for sale. They look at pretty items on many other shelves, and notice medicine on the back shelves. They even see a few toys on some low shelves in the center of the store.

There is a wind-up dog that walks and barks when you wind the key. Buddy picks it up, looks at it, smiling, and holds it up to his daddy. Daddy winds it up and lets it walk across a low shelf.

"You wouldn't want a doggie like that would you?" John asks, winking at Nancy.

"No, I don't think he would," his mother says.

"Oh, yes, yes, I would. Could I get him, daddy?" Buddy begs.

"Well, I guess you can get him," John drawls, smiling and hugging Buddy. "Pick him up and let mommy carry him while I show you something else."

Daddy picks Buddy up and places him on one of the tall round stools in front of the soda fountain. He and Nancy sit on either side of Buddy. Daddy asks, "How would you like to have a big scoop of ice cream in a cone?"

"I don't know, is it good?" Buddy asks.

"How about giving us each a cone with strawberry ice cream" John asks the counter man, who wears a white military-style cap and a big white apron.

"You bet." he answers, smiling at Buddy, as he picks up a pointed cone and places a large scoop of ice cream in it, pink and yummy looking. He hands the ice cream cone to Buddy, then fixes two more, handing one to Nancy, then to John.

"This is my birthday." Buddy tells the counter man.

"How old are you?" the man asks. "Can you show me on your fingers?" Buddy holds up 4 fingers. He almost drops the big cone, but gets a little help from his mother, who is holding several napkins, 'just in case' they are needed.

"Umm, good," Buddy says, after licking the ice cream.

When the ice cream is gone, Nancy wipes Buddy's face and hands as well as she can with dry paper napkins, and John leads Buddy to the candy counter.

"Let us have one of those chocolate B-B Bat Suckers," he says to the man behind the candy counter. "And 10 cents worth of gumdrops."

Turning back to Buddy, John says "We'll have the gumdrops to share with Grandma and Uncle Alfred. Save your B-B Bat until you get home."

John takes their candy to the cash register, where a young lady rings up their purchases: one cent for the sucker, ten cents for the gumdrops, the three five-cent ice cream cones, and the wind-up doggie.

The man at the ice cream counter shouts to the lady, "Don't charge him for one of the cones. It is a birthday gift to that little man there." John pays seventy-three cents, counting fifty cents for the toy dog and two cents tax.

When they return to Grandma's house, John announces that Rags will have to stay behind when they leave for Kansas City. Alfred loves Rags, and offers to keep him. John tells Buddy that he has the wind-up doggie and he can play with it until they can get another dog in Kansas City. Buddy fusses and cries about it that first night, but plays a lot with the toy dog. He starts calling it Ragsy.

There is another problem. They need to sell the car. It is fine for local driving, but it is using a lot of oil and John knows it would not make it half-way across the country. So, he puts a "For Sale" sign on the car's side window. A few days later a young man comes by and wants to buy the car. John sells the car for $150.00, a pretty good price. That money and some savings from his job gives them enough to buy train tickets and food to eat on the way, and still have a little left over.

By the first of September John, Nancy and Buddy are packed up, ready to go see Grandpa Weideman and his new wife Minerva in Kansas City. John's brother Alfred drives them to the train station. They travel on the Great Northern Railway Transcontinental Railroad that goes from the Pacific Ocean to Chicago. In order to go southeast to Kansas City, they have to switch trains in Glacier, Colorado.

The train stops at stations along the way, taking on coal and water for the steam engine, freight, mail and passengers. The trip takes the biggest part of a week. But it is a beautiful time of the year to travel across the country, with the trees turning red, yellow and orange on the hills, watching the Rocky Mountains as they pass by, and going through tunnels at times.

The train ride is tiring, but something to remember. Buddy will remember it for a long time afterwards.

CHAPTER 3

Kansas City Life

At the Kansas City Union Station the family takes a taxi to 1224 East 16th Street, where Grandpa and Grandma Weideman live. It is late afternoon when they climb the stairs up the terrace and onto the porch, hoping someone is home. Soon a lady comes from next door asking who they are looking for.

John says, "We are looking for my father. His name is Julius Weideman. Does he live here?"

"Well, you must be John," the lady says.

"Julius told me you would be coming soon. He got the telegram you sent from the train station in Boise. I'm Minerva, Julius' wife. I was just having an afternoon cup of coffee with my neighbor, Mrs. Blumm. Come on in, the door's not locked."

Once inside, John introduces Nancy and Warren to Grandma Weideman, saying, "We call Warren 'Buddy' now."

Minerva asks Nancy to sit down.   Then she kneels down and holds out her hands to Buddy, saying, "Come see your new grandma. Grandpa will be off work soon."

Buddy creeps closer and lets her give him a hug. He says, "I have another grandma where we used to live. She made me a birthday cake when I was 4 years old. I had a dog there, too."

"What do you know about that!" Minerva exclaims. "You are a good-looking boy, and such a lively talker. You'll have to tell us all about your doggie, but, listen; I think I hear grandpa coming up the stairs. Won't he be surprised to see you all here already? Here, Buddy, hide behind this door and pop out and say, 'Hi, grandpa' when he comes in the front door."

Julius beams with pride as he catches a glimpse of his son and Nancy.

Then Buddy pops out from behind the door and shouts, "Boo Grandpa!" He catches grandpa off guard, and Julius nearly falls down with his black metal lunch bucket.

"Wow! What a surprise," he exclaims, setting his lunch bucket on a chair.

"Who is this little monkey that's trying to scare the daylights out of me?"

At that, Buddy runs to grandpa and says, "It's me, Buddy, grandpa," and he nearly jumps into grandpa's open arms. He is having a wonderful time.

Grandpa sets Buddy on his lap awhile and asks him about his trip on the train.   Then Buddy tells grandpa about Rags and Ragsy, and shows the toy dog to him. They play with Ragsy awhile as grandpa talks to John and Nancy, and Minerva goes to fix supper. Nancy gets up soon to go help Minerva. But a large pot of navy beans and ham is already warm and waiting on the stove as

Minerva pops a pan of cornbread into her gas oven. Nancy sets places for everyone at the table and pours glasses of milk. She sets a bowl of butter on the table, as well as some honey.

John and Nancy plan to stay with his parents for a few weeks. John starts working with Julius in construction. However, construction jobs become scarce. People have a hard time getting loans, and some of the banks meet financial ruin that next year, 1929. It seems that the family is "stuck in time", getting what little work they can, and living together. John and Nancy begin to get depressed. John brings home beer and he and Nancy pull off to themselves, drinking up some of their scarce money. This does not set well with Minerva.

Grandpa Julius enjoys Buddy immensely. Every evening they play together. Grandpa crosses his legs, and Buddy sits on Grandpa's foot to "ride the pony." They play catch with a ball, and Buddy laughs as grandpa makes a bumble bee sound, moving his pointer finger around and poking Buddy's tummy, saying, "Gotcha!"

During the day Nancy helps Minerva with the housework. She encourages Buddy to run in the house because the yard is terraced and dangerous for children to play on. Sometimes they walk to a near-by park where he can play, but many days are too wet or cold to play outside. Buddy needs to keep up the strength in his legs they had worked so hard for him to get. However, running in the house seems to Minerva like rowdiness. She can not comprehend Buddy's poor physical condition at birth. Therefore tension develops between Nancy and Minerva.

CHAPTER 4

River Life

By May of 1930 Nancy begs John to find a way for them to have a home of their own. John says, "We can afford to buy a large tent and live in it until we can build a house. But land costs more money than we have. People in the neighborhood are talking about the land north of the Missouri River, which is free."

Nancy answers, "I'm willing to live in the tent on the river bank and help you build a house. I'm used to hard work, you know."

John borrows his dad's truck and takes the tent and the belongings they brought with them from Idaho over to the place where they will build. Nancy and Buddy go with him. Grandpa is sad to see them go, but he knew it had to happen. John and Nancy get the tent set up. He takes the truck back to his dad, and rides the trolley back to the river area. John has to walk a mile after he gets off the trolley.

This free land is between the Missouri River and the dyke that protects the small village of Harlem, close to the small town of North Kansas City. People in the village of Harlem are rather poor also, and built small houses. But, because they lived in the village, they had to pay for their land.

John buys some lumber and other needed supplies from a lumber yard in North Kansas City. They deliver the lumber and agree to let John make payments on it a little each month. John looks for work in "North-Town," as it is called. But jobs are extremely scarce. Their family has to eat, so John makes fishing poles, one for himself, and a small one for Buddy. They fish every day so they have meat to eat. They brought a few staples with them. They start selling fish to some of the neighbors. This gives them money for other foods from the small variety store in Harlem.

Since they live very close to the river, and Buddy is so active now, John decides that Buddy should learn to swim. John jumps into the river and swims out a ways and back.

He calls Buddy to him and says, "Son, you watched me swim; now I want you to swim like I did."

"O.K.", Buddy says.

John picks him up, carries him out a ways, drops him in the water, and says, "Swim."

Buddy takes to the water like a duck! Nancy is watching from a chair in front of the house. It is a big relief for John and Nancy to see how well Buddy swims on his first try. He really likes swimming, and comes up smiling.

"That was fun!" Buddy shouts.

Building the house goes well. John's father had given him several tools when they moved to the river area. That is a wonderful help. They have the house framed in a few days, with two doors and two windows. But there is just tar paper on the outside of the house, with no paint. The wooden roof is covered with rolls of roofing. In a few weeks time, they have a house of their own. They heat the house with coal in a pot-bellied stove, cook on a kerosene stove, and use kerosene lamps for light. There is no plumbing in the house. Once a week they bathe in a galvanized tub filled with hot water heated on the stove. An out house is their toilet. John hires someone to build them a cistern in the yard with a hand pump. They can now wash clothes in a galvanized tub and rinse in a second one, and then hang the clothes on a clothesline tied between two trees.

After the house is built, John turns his efforts to building a boat so they can fish in the deeper water and catch more fish. Building a boat is quite difficult, but there are plenty of trees around them. John cuts down trees he can shape into a boat. Buddy "helps" with putting tar on the boat to seal out water—until a dab of it gets caught in Buddy's brown wavy hair, causing Nancy to give him his first haircut.

John decides to teach Buddy how to tie knots so he can help make a net to catch the fish. It is tedious for his little fingers, but Buddy is happy to be helping his daddy again. They continue fishing on the river bank with poles until the net and the boat are done.

Some of the neighbor men help John build the boat. One man is named Happy Zubie. Happy is a bachelor who does odd jobs for people. He always wears a mashed down fishing hat over his slightly graying hair. He is a happy-go-lucky person that most people like to have around.

Another man in the area who comes to help build the boat is Billy Scott. He is a young man, without parents, and works at the Harlem variety store during the day. But he helps John in the evenings. Billy is a thoughtful kind of person. He wants to be useful wherever he can. Billy is red headed, but lacks the quick temper often thought to go with red hair. It isn't all work, because Nancy invites the two men to join them for supper most evenings while they work on the boat. Fish, potatoes, and beans are plentiful.

Once the boat is done, including oars to propel it, the men start using a strong, course, but rather thin rope to

tie knots that form a pattern making a large net that can catch fish. They also make a trotline using a strong fishing line that can be strung out over a long distance with many shorter lines dangling down from it, with hooks along the short lines. Happy shows John how to do these things. He has lived just across the dyke from the river for many years. John and Buddy fish in the boat every day. It turns out to be a very busy summer.

By fall John sells fish each evening. Carp sells for 5 cents a pound. Catfish, bass, and other good fish sell for 15 cents a pound. John offers to clean the fish for an extra 5 cents a fish.

John and Nancy don't have much money for Buddy's 5th birthday in September, 1930. Nancy is able to make a birthday cake, white with white powdered-sugar icing for Buddy's birthday. Nancy and John sing "Happy Birthday" to Buddy before they eat the cake. They take him for a walk after supper, down a lane to a neighbor's house, where they had seen a dog with several puppies. Nancy knows the lady who answers the door.

"Hello, Jane" Nancy says. "We've been looking for a puppy for Buddy."

"Come inside," Jane says. "Sit down, I've been meaning to visit you ever since I saw you at the store. You say you want a puppy?"

"Yes," Nancy says. "We had to leave our other dog behind with relatives when we moved to Missouri. Do you still have one that you want to give away?"

Jane's daughter, Sara Jane, is peeking around the corner from the next room.

Jane says, "Come here, Sara Jane, and go get the puppy for these people to see." Sara Jane runs out the back door and comes back quickly with a fuzzy brown puppy. Buddy runs over to her and pets the puppy.

"Would you like to have this puppy, Buddy?" inquires Jane, smiling and winking at Nancy.

"Yes, yes, he's so soft.   He looks like a baby bear," Buddy manages.

"Then you can have him," Jane says.

John and Nancy get up and thank Jane for the puppy. Buddy also thanks her and he carries the puppy home. Nancy makes the puppy a bed in a low box.

After Buddy plays with the new puppy for a while, he puts him in his new bed and says "Go to sleep, Bear."

Even with fish for sale, there are many things the family needs that they can't buy.   President Franklin Delano Roosevelt has set up some plans to help people during these times that are so bad financially. There are places where used clothes and food are stored, and given to those who have no jobs. Besides these places, there are jobs undertaken to help communities, where people are paid by the government to do the work. John decides to go to North Kansas City to inquire about these things. He comes home and tells Nancy they should go get some of the clothes and food. They take Buddy with them on the trolley. The clothes closet does not have any shoes Buddy's size. He has outgrown the moccasins he received from Chief Brave Hunter's family on his third birthday, but his feet are pretty tough from going bare-foot all summer.

John continues fishing every day and selling fish in the evenings.

In November John goes back to the clothes closet. This time he finds a pair of shoes for Buddy. They are high tops with buttons to fasten the shoes. Buddy has to learn to use a metal button hook, which has a wooden handle with a hook on the other end. He pokes the hook through a button hole on one side of the shoe and pulls the toggle-type button through the hole. There are six buttons on each shoe. John also finds two pairs of long stockings for Buddy (one black pair, the other tan).   That's what the young boys and girls wore.

It is harder to fish in the winter, but they still manage to catch and sell some, helping with the kerosene and coal they have to buy. John usually manages to bring some beer home. He and Nancy seem to "need" it.

In the spring of 1931 things look a little brighter, with no need to buy coal, and the fishing got better. One day Happy Zubie stops to talk to John and Buddy while they are fishing from the bank.

Happy says to Buddy, "Your daddy is quite a fisherman."

Buddy says, "I'm quite a fisher boy, too."

Happy laughs and says, "You sure are at that!" Many times after that Happy calls Buddy 'Fisher Boy' instead of calling him Buddy.

Buddy tells him one day, "I'm going to catch a fish bigger than the fish my daddy catches."

"Oh, you'll have to let me see it when you do," Happy says. That encourages Buddy to fish on the river bank awhile each day after helping his daddy pull in the trotline and pull in the net full of fish. Buddy is getting pretty good at helping bait the trotline. They use a small net to catch little fish for bait. They have a place in back of their house where they pitch all the peelings and scraps from their food, and coffee grounds to "grow" earthworms.

Buddy swims in the river awhile every day. He is quite a good swimmer by now.

CHAPTER 5

Grade School Years

Buddy can't go to school until he is six and almost seven years old in 1932, because of the cut-off date for entering school. Buddy is very happy when his mother takes him to school the first day, showing him how to walk to and from school. Some other children who also live below the dyke walk with him after the first day. There are steps up one side of the dyke and down the other. It is a half mile to school in Harlem. Buddy feels like a big boy now.

Harlem school has eight grades in one room. The children play games at recess and at lunch time after they eat. The girls like to play jump-rope. Buddy asks to play jump rope with them. They let him join in, turning the rope for others until his turn to jump. When a person misses, they have to be a rope turner. The girls like Buddy. He is cute and easy to get along with. Some other boys play jump rope too, but most play baseball. Buddy likes to play dodge ball with boys and girls. It is a lot of fun playing on the playground at school. He likes to learn, too. He especially likes to add sums. For lunch, Buddy's sandwich is sometimes filled with cold mashed potatoes. Other times it is a bean sandwich. Buddy always fishes in the boat with his father before going to school and helps sell the fish after he comes home.

Bear eagerly jumps up on Buddy after school, hoping for a few pets and maybe a race down the hill. Sometimes Bear goes to school with Buddy, frolicking with whichever child he can coax into playing, throwing a stick for him to

fetch, or running a race with him. When the school bell
rings Bear knows it is time to go home.

When school is out for the summer there is more time
to fish, which Buddy likes to do. He is also getting better
and better at swimming in that wide, swift Missouri River.

Sometimes on the weekends, excursion boats come by,
playing music. They are loaded with people who pay for a
scenic ride. They eat, drink, and dance on the deck.
Buddy and some of the other boys swim out close to the
boats to take a look. People throw coins out for the boys
to catch. The boys have to be good "catchers" so the coins
don't go down into the water and sink out of sight. Fisher
Boy and his friends have a great time swimming. Some of
them say that he swims like a fish.

PLANE WRECK

Very close to Harlem and North Kansas City there is a
rather new airport named Kansas City Municipal Airport.
Planes fly overhead several times a day. One day, just as
John and Buddy are pulling their boat up to the bank,
they hear a loud noise. They turn and watch in horror as a
small plane noses down into the river between the two
bridges close to their house.

John says, "Buddy, get out of the boat! Hurry to the
house. Tell your mother to run to the store and call the
fire department and police. You go with her, and then
stay with her at the house." Happy also hears the noise.

He calls to another man who is cutting his grass next door.

Happy yells, "Come on, Harry, let's get to John's boat and go see about that plane. People might be hurt."

John is backing the boat out, but waits for the two as they run across the dyke. As they approach the plane, they plan to get the pilot out, but as the boat touches the plane, it is obvious the pilot is dead.

The best thing they can do is to nudge the plane toward the shore. By the time they get the wrecked plane stabilized at the river bank, help arrives from the calls Nancy made.

The authorities discover it is a mail plane, so they called the Kansas City Post Office. A police escort takes the Postal authorities to the scene. Mail in bags totaling 100 pounds is saved.

The quick thinking of John and the neighbors makes news in the Kansas City Times newspaper. They send a photographer, who captures the scene, with John and Happy in the picture.

BAREFOOTED BOYS

When fall arrives Buddy goes to second grade.

Buddy sits on the end of the front row for their class photo. He shows the photographer his dimple!

The boys do not wear shoes in the summer, and some of them start school without shoes. This is common because it is hard to keep buying shoes for growing children.

But again, when it turns cold, John gets Buddy a pair of shoes from the clothes closet. While he is in town he inquires at the unemployment office, without luck. For John, drinking while fishing becomes a way of life.

Buddy brings home decent grade cards in second grade. He likes spelling very much, because he is good at it, as well as addition and subtraction.

The teacher rings a bell from the doorway when it is time for the children to come inside. The children beg to be allowed to ring the bell. Buddy has several turns. There is always something exciting and interesting going on at school.

CURLS IN THE INKWELL

By the time Buddy is in the third grade he is an excellent reader. He still helps his father with fishing before and after school. But then, he likes fishing. He still has that dream of catching a great big fish!

One day John buys Buddy a bag of marbles and shows him how to place them in a circle drawn in the dirt, then take a tall, (a large marble), and see how many marbles he can shoot out of the ring. Each person keeps the marbles they shoot out, until the game is over. Buddy takes the marbles to school and plays marbles with the other boys.

At school this year they are taught to use ink pens. The pens have wooden handles and metal ink tips, which fit into slots at the end of the handles. They dip the metal tip into the ink well that is built into their school desks. Buddy begins thinking that a little red-headed girl is pretty cute. She sits in front of Buddy. Lorene is the Baptist preacher's daughter. She has long curly hair. Buddy gets a strange notion. He grabs one of Lorene's curls and dips it into his inkwell. He barely gets it in the well, but there is ink on it. Lorene feels a slight pull, turns around, and figures out what Buddy has done. She lets out a little cry. The teacher then notices there is trouble and goes to find out what happened.

Lorene whimpers, "Buddy put my curly hair in his inkwell."

The surprised teacher asks Buddy, "Did you do that?" Buddy nods his head and the other children snicker.

"Why, I'm surprised at you, Buddy. That is not a nice thing to do." She takes Lorene to the water basin that is on a stand by the front door, and uses a towel to wash her hair off.

Buddy begins to feel quite bad about what he has done, because he really likes Lorene, and just wanted to get her attention. The teacher calls Buddy up to her desk, bends Buddy's hand back and gives him a couple of taps on the wrist with her twelve-inch ruler. It is not meant to make him cry, but it sure does embarrass him.

The teacher asks Buddy, "Don't you want to apologize to Lorene?" Buddy nods.

Then he says, "I'm sorry."

THE BIG CATCH?

In fourth grade, Buddy plays jacks with the girls. He also plays baseball with the boys now. There is always the fishing before and after school.

Buddy likes the catfish best for eating. But sometimes he gets a little tired of eating so much fish.

Buddy makes a "big catch" one day after school. He catches a 4-pounder. It is a big fish for a boy. Buddy shows his big fish to his parents, who admire it and take a picture of it.

Then he crosses the dyke to show Happy.

"That's a fair-sized fish alright! Congratulations!" says Happy.

"It may not be the biggest one I ever catch, but I like this one well enough to clean it myself."

THE RIVER IS RISING!

One morning, when John and Buddy go out to fish before school, they notice that the river has risen about a foot. It has been raining for three days. Other times, the river rose and got rather close to their house. This time, it seems to be coming up faster. So, they decided it isn't safe to go out in the boat that day. Buddy goes on to school. After school he hurries home and finds water almost up to their door. John and Nancy have put their tent on the other side of the levy in Happy's yard. They are in the process of carrying clothes, bedding and food up over the dyke in case the water gets into their house. Buddy and Bear follow along. Buddy carries as much as he can. When they finish, Happy invites them in to eat supper with him. Then they go to bed in the tent. In the morning, they go back over the dyke to see how far up the water came. The water is up about two feet inside of their house!

John says, "Places up the river from us must have had even harder rains than we had in order for the river to come up so fast."

Nancy is worried. She says, "Some of our things might get washed away with that much water in the house. How many days do you think it will last, John?"

"Several days, hard to tell exactly now, Nan." he answers. "But we'll be O.K. If things wash away, then maybe we didn't need them anyway. I tied the boat up really good. We sure do need it."

They go back to the tent, and John goes to the variety store in Harlem to buy several bottles of bleach for cleaning up the house when the water leaves. Buddy goes on to school every day, and finally, on the fifth day, the water is out of the house, but still in the yard. They wait until the next day, a Saturday, to go back to the house. Some furniture is turned over and very dirty, but nothing seems to be missing. They spend Saturday and Sunday cleaning all the furniture and walls and floors. They stay in the tent until Tuesday to let the house dry out. Finally, after school on Tuesday, they all work together carrying items back home. Happy helps them fold up the tent and put it away. Floods are events they have to expect while living so close to the river.

FIFTH GRADE

In fifth grade Buddy learns about his state of Missouri, and wishes he could go see other parts of the state. His parents talk about the trip the family took on the train when they came to Missouri. Buddy doesn't remember very much about the trip.

One of the bridges that cross the river near the Weidemans' house has tracks so trains can go from Kansas City to other parts of the country. It is named Hannibal Bridge. When tall boats want to go down the river, a watchman turns a section of the bridge around so the boats can go through. Then he turns it back around so the trains can go across when they come. This is an interesting place to live. On the other side of their house there is a bridge where automobiles cross the river, as well as trolley cars. It is called the A.S.B. Bridge. Sometimes John takes Buddy with him up by the bridge where they can catch a trolley car and ride into North Kansas City to buy groceries. Times are still pretty hard financially, but those rides on the trolley are special. Buddy wants to ride a real train again some day.

Right now Buddy is content to help his dad sell fish. Most of the time they row up the Kansas River (called the Kaw River). They are rowing against the stream. Then they drop their net into the river and catch fish as they drift back down stream into the Missouri River and on down to their house.

John and Buddy build a huge crate made of slat-like boards to hold the fish they catch. The crate stays in the

river, anchored down, and has a lid that they can open to
dip fish out with a small hand-held net when the people
come to buy.   Buyers come from Kansas City and North-
Town.   News spreads by word of mouth about the nice
supply of fresh fish, at reasonable prices.

RIVER WHIRLPOOL

When Buddy is eleven years old, it is an exceptionally
cold winter, making the purchase of coal difficult.   John
gets an idea.   He climbs up on the Hannibal Bridge where
the trains go, loaded down with coal.   He is able to climb
aboard a coal car, taking a shovel with him.   He shovels
several large lumps of coal down onto the ground.   Then
he jumps off the train and he and Buddy break up the
pieces and carry them home in buckets.   This happens
several times through the winter.

A friend gives Buddy an old pair of roller skates.   There
is no place to use them, so he takes the rollers off and
uses them as ice skates on a small pond-like area where
water collects and freezes.   Other children use ice skates
and have fun on the small "pond" also.

When summer arrives, Buddy swims clear across the
wide Missouri River.   This is quite a big accomplishment
for an eleven year old boy.   Right at the Kansas City
Municipal Airport, which is next to Harlem, the river is
extra wide because that is where the Kansas River empties
into the Missouri River.

Several boys and girls swim in the river close to the
shore.   A group of them are swimming together when
Buddy disappears under the water and doesn't come up
right away.

"Buddy, Buddy!" the kids shout, "Where are you?"

About that time Buddy pops up, gasping and scared!
Bobby, Harry, Sara Jane and Alice are very glad to see
him surface.   They gather around as Bobby asks, "What
happened to you?"

Buddy, spitting out water, and catching his breath,
answers "I got caught in a whirl-pool.   It took me to the
bottom of the river, then suddenly shot me right back up.

You know, we've heard about them, but I hadn't ever been in a whirlpool before. That was scary!"

"Could you see anything?" Sara Jane wanted to know.

"I closed my eyes and had a hard time holding my breath that long." Buddy replies. "I sure don't want to get in any more whirlpools."

"I wouldn't know what to do if I got caught in one," says Bobby.

"Boy! I learned that if it happens again I won't fight it, I'll let it take me all the way down, because I know it will kick me right back up again," says Buddy.

SCOUT TROOP AT HARLEM CHURCH

When Buddy is twelve years old he starts going to a small Baptist Church in Harlem. That's the church where Rev. Hamblen is pastor. His daughter, Lorene, is the red-headed girl in Buddy's class at school. She and Buddy are in Sunday School class together and they become friends there. Buddy teases Lorene, saying, "Keep your curls out of my inkwell."

Mr. Virgil Bower, the Harlem School's seventh grade teacher, is also the scoutmaster, whose troop of Boy Scouts met at Harlem Baptist Church. Buddy goes to the scout meetings every week and works on projects that earn him merit badges. Buddy does quite well, gradually ascending to higher ranks. He makes beaded items and other handicrafts. John teaches Buddy how to develop film and print the photos the way John did in Boise. That earns Buddy a merit badge too.

Mr. Bower takes Buddy and some other boys "under his wing," buying scout uniforms for them and helping them earn money. He takes a different boy each week to mow his yard with his push mower. Mr. Bower lives about 9 miles north of North Kansas City, in a nice subdivision called Green Haven. The yard is smooth and easy to cut. He gives the scout a dollar for cutting the yard. Mrs. Bower gives the boy lunch after he mows the lawn.

A NEW FRIEND

Buddy goes to the K.C. Municipal Airport and sells tickets to their big Boy Scout Round-Up, held in Kansas City every year. Selling tickets to the Round-Up makes some money for their troop. One day, while Buddy is selling tickets to people at the airport, he meets a boy just a little older than he is. The boy, named Ralph, is helping his step-father load up trash from a TWA airplane. They are paid to get the airplanes ready for their next flight. Ralph drops a bag of cardboard cups and small plates, scattering them around on the blacktop. Buddy, always the good scout, helps Ralph pick them up. Ralph is very thankful for the help. His step-father is a rather impatient man. Buddy introduces himself and says he lives on the river, near Harlem. Ralph says, "We live close to your house. We just moved from Kansas City to a rented house here on the river so my step-father could take the job at TWA. Buddy says, "Great, why don't you come over to my house and go swimming with me and my dog, Bear?" Ralph says, "I will, when I can."

BUDDY, THE EAGLE SCOUT

Buddy continues working through his scouting ranks. He still needs some additional merit badges that he can earn by going to Osceola Scout Camp, including diving. When swimming at the river, Buddy had no place to dive. John would climb up on the cement support of the A.S.B. Bridge, and then dive from there. But he always said that it was too dangerous for Buddy. Mr. Bower pays his way to camp, and also goes to the camp as a counselor. There, Buddy finishes his requirements, including diving and techniques of life saving, thereby becoming an Eagle Scout, the highest rank in scouting!

Scoutmaster Virgil Bower is extremely proud of Buddy. Buddy is his *very first Eagle Scout!* There will be an impressive ceremony called an Eagle Court of Honor in January at the big auditorium in Kansas City for him and other scouts from the area that have attained the rank of Eagle Scout.

Mr. Bower is an excellent role model and mentor for Buddy. They will remain friends throughout life.

BAPTISM IN THE RIVER

Buddy continues going to church every Sunday. A few months later another important thing happens to Buddy. Buddy is saved and becomes a Christian. He is baptized by Rev. Hamblen in the river. The church people walk from the church to the river where they sing a hymn. The preacher prays, then leads Buddy and other new Christians into the river and baptizes them, one at a time, by tipping them backwards into the water and raising them back up, like John the Baptist did in the Bible.

CHAPTER 5

High School Years

Buddy rides the bus to North Kansas City High School. He really likes string class, a special class where violin, viola, cello, and string bass are taught. In string class there is a pretty girl that he likes a lot. She is shy, with a pretty smile and curly brown hair. She plays the violin and he plays the cello. They also are in orchestra together.

Buddy joins the high school marching band as well, by learning to play the school's baritone horn. The marching band members wear purple and gold uniforms, play in the stands and put on a show at half time at the football games. Buddy wants to take advantage of all the opportunities he has. This makes life more interesting.

NEW GIRL, NEW NAME

The violinist he likes is named Leondine Patterson. Buddy nick-names her Dene, and she calls him Bud. Bud walks Dene to class whenever possible, without being late for his own class. Dene rides a bus ten miles to a subdivision called Evanston Place, north of North Kansas City.

Bud likes to bring the school's cello home with him on Wednesdays and Fridays so he can take it to church with him and play the hymns along with the pianist when the congregation sings. He also could practice that way.

Another class Bud likes is algebra. Another cute girl named Bonnie sits next to him in that class. He sometimes helps her with her algebra problems.

One of Bud's friends, named James Spencer, sometimes called Jimmy, has a used bike. His parents are going to get him a new one for his birthday. Bud decides he will find a way to earn money to buy the used bicycle. Five dollars seems like a lot of money. He takes the trolley into Kansas City to look for places where a fifteen-year-old boy can be hired. A hamburger stand on Sixth Street, where hamburgers, French fries, and soda are the only items for sale, gives him a chance to work. Hamburgers are five cents each or six for 25 cents. Bud learns just how long to fry the hamburgers on each side, and brown the bun on the grill. He also figures out just how dark to make the French fries. Bud works on weekends and a few evenings. Finally, he has enough money to buy the bicycle. After he gets the bike, he rides it to school on the days he doesn't want to take the cello home.

Bud also rides his bike to work at the hamburger stand, saving bus fare. Trolleys are being changed over to buses in Kansas City and North Kansas City. All the tracks in the streets are being removed. Bud is glad they are removing the tracks, but it causes some difficulty getting around the work zones on his bike.

Bud's dad gets a job with the Work Projects Administration, known as W.P.A.

It is a program where the U.S. government pays workers to build things. They are building a football stadium and track at the North Kansas City High School.

John and Bud still catch fish, but now they are busier than ever, and happy to be making more money. John buys something nice for the family with some of his pay from W.P.A. It is a battery operated radio, about half the size of a breadbox. They listen to it every evening, and sometimes in the morning.

Bud and Ralph become good friends. Ralph tells Bud, "I went to two years of high school at Manuel High School in Kansas City, but my step-dad thinks I need to work instead of going to school. So, I'm looking for a job."

Bud says, "With the war going on in Europe, a lot of American men are signing up to join the Army, just in case we get into the war. My dad says that jobs should be opening up more because of that. So maybe you'll have some luck soon."

Ralph goes swimming with Bud. He is amazed at how well Bud swims. He makes it look so easy. He just stretches out and slides into the water. Ralph plays with Bear more than actually swimming. Bear loves to retrieve sticks thrown into the river.

Ralph soon gets a job delivering telegrams for Postal Telegraph. He uses his bicycle and delivers them all over North Kansas City and Harlem.

Grandpa Julius Weideman has his wife, Minerva, write a letter to John and Nancy asking how they are doing. In it she says, "Grandpa sure misses Buddy."

Bud writes a letter back to them and tells them about being in orchestra and band, and that he has a job at a hamburger stand. Bud and his grandparents visit each other and write letters back and forth for the rest of his Grandparents' lives.

Just before the Christmas break the orchestra gives a concert. That evening after the concert Bud tells Dene's parents, Mr. and Mrs. Patterson, about the nick name he gave Leondine.

Mr. Patterson smiles and says, "I think that is a cute nick name for her."

Mrs. Patterson says, "I think so, too."

Bud asks Dene to go with him to store his cello in the band room. Dene's sisters, Louise and Winnie, ask to go with them to see the band room.

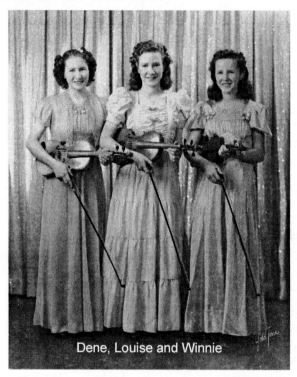
Dene, Louise and Winnie

Louise will be in orchestra next year with her violin. So up to the second floor they go. The halls are dim because only a few lights are needed.

On the way back to the auditorium where the girls' parents are waiting for them, Bud and Dene hang back a little, holding hands, and Bud stops and gives Dene her first kiss—rather quickly. Then they catch up with her sisters. Their little brother, Eldon, stayed with the girls' parents, Lisle and Hazel. The Pattersons are proud of the way the orchestra performs. The orchestra will also play for graduation in May.

Bud invites the Pattersons to his Eagle Scout Court of Honor that is coming up on January 3, 1941, at the Kansas City Auditorium.

Before they part, Bud gives Dene a Christmas gift, which he has her unwrap. It is a bottle of Evening In Paris perfume, which is all the rage these days, in a royal blue crown-shaped bottle with a tassel. The tag on it says "Greetings Dene. To a great girl. With Love, Bud W." Dene is rather taken aback. She is realizing that Bud likes her a lot. She really likes him, too. Her smile and "Thank You" make him very happy.

When the day comes for the Eagle Scout Court of Honor, Mr. Patterson decides they will go to watch it, since Eldon will be in scouts some day. Mr. Bower picks Bud up and takes him to the K.C. Auditorium for the event. Bud has arranged to meet the Pattersons at the entrance. He helps them find their seats, and then goes with Mr. Bower to find the other scouts.

It is a very impressive service. They make much of the fact that Bud is Mr. Bower's *first Eagle Scout*, and Mr. Bower tells how proud he is of Bud. He receives a pin for his Scout uniform, plus one for his mother. After the service the Pattersons look at the awards and pins. They tell Bud how proud they are of him. Bud takes the other pin home to his mother, who tells Bud she is very proud of him and she is sorry she didn't feel like going to see him get the award. John also comes into the room and looks at the pin and his award. He is proud also.

The Pattersons also go every year to the Boy Scout Round-up at the Auditorium in K.C. The scouts present very elaborate and beautiful activities on the large hall floor. They use flags similar to the ones girls use in high school bands, and sometimes they use streamers to make displays. There are patriotic presentations, including making a large U.S. flag. They do some Indian dances with full costumes and tom-toms, and Indian calls. It is always a magnificent display of talent.

One afternoon in June, 1941, Bud rides his bicycle out to Evanston Place to visit Dene. It is a ten-mile ride over many long hills. He and the three girls sit in the yard and talk awhile and have some lemonade. Bud enjoys petting their cow that is staked out in the yard. He also enjoys seeing the dozen chickens in the fenced area that includes a chicken coop with nests for laying hens. Each child has a hen for a pet. The chicken squats down to let the child pick her up. They also have a big garden with corn, beans, peas and radishes.

Their home has electricity, and their cistern pump is in the kitchen sink, rather than outside the house. They use galvanized tubs for baths. They also have an outhouse. After the nice visit Bud thanks the girls for the lemonade, and says he enjoyed the visit. Then he rides his bike back home.

A few days later Bud talks to a Hershey candy bar salesman at the Harlem store, while Bud is there buying bread for his parents. The candy salesman wants Bud to go with him on his candy route to several cities delivering the sweets.

"I can use the extra help with our promotion of Heath Bars," he says.

After Bud takes the bread home, he asks his parents for their opinion. They think it would be a good opportunity for him. Bud heads back to the store and tells the candy salesman he can go. Bud goes to the hamburger stand that evening, and tells them he has to quit because he has a higher paying job. The next morning at 8:00 a.m. Bud meets the salesman, Sam Jones, at the Harlem store again, taking a small suitcase of clothes with him. They are gone the rest of that week and another week before they return to Harlem. Bud likes the work, but he misses swimming in the river. Also, fishing has to "take a back seat."

After the trip, Bud has the week-end off. He rides out to see Dene again on Saturday. Mr. Patterson admires the distance Bud rides in the hot sun. He invites Bud inside to play some Chinese checkers with the girls. "Can you stay for lunch and wait awhile until it gets a little cooler before you go home?" Lisle asks.

"Sure," Bud says.

They discuss Bud's new job, and Mr. Patterson thinks it is probably a good one. Bud has brought some Heath Bars to give to the family. They put them in the refrigerator before eating them, since it is such a hot day.

FIRE!

One evening as Nancy is preparing dinner, she suddenly cries out in distress.

"Fire!" she shouts.

Nancy had been depressed and drinking quite a bit that day. She splashed some grease from a skillet onto the kerosene burner, which flared up suddenly, catching the window curtain on fire.

"Help, Fire," she yells out the door where John and Bud are.

They come running in, and see the blazing curtain turn the wall brown and smoke up the whole room. John grabs a bucket and runs to the cistern pump to fill it. Bud grasps the garbage bucket, empties it outside and then fills it full of water. They get a bucket brigade going. Nancy uses the broom to try to beat out some of the flames. A small cabinet catches on fire. There are legal documents, including their wedding certificate and birth certificates in one of the drawers. Luckily, they douse the cabinet quickly enough to save most of those important papers. When the fire is finally out, there is a terrible mess to clean up, and everyone is exhausted. The potatoes Nancy was frying have to be thrown away.

John says, "Let's leave the mess until we take a walk to the Harlem store and get something for sandwiches. We can have sandwiches and ice cream to eat instead of supper. When you do stupid things like that, you see what happens."

This doesn't make Nancy feel any better, but she changes her dress and goes with them.

John and Bud wait outside for Nancy. John is reminded of Bud's 4th birthday when Bud had his first ice cream.

"Do you remember your first ice cream cone, Fisher Boy?"

Bud answers, "I do remember the taste of it, but I don't remember any real details, except that I got Ragsy then. I still have him."

The walk to the store is a welcome relief for the family. They get a half pound of bologna and a loaf of bread. They sit on a bench outside the store. After they finish eating the sandwiches, they have some ice cream. They eat chocolate-covered vanilla ice cream on a stick. They each have two, but Bud's second one is solid chocolate. They then return to clean up the mess from the fire. Even though the house smells smoky, they are quite relieved to get to bed that night.

On the fourth of July, Ralph comes to see Bud, who is home from his second trip with Mr. Jones. Ralph has some fire crackers, which he lets Bud help him shoot off. Ralph puts a little larger one inside a tin can, with the fuse sticking out. When he lights the fuse, the can flies into the air, landing in a cluster of cottonwood tree branches. He also had sparklers, but they decide that those are not as much fun as fire crackers. Lastly, they each shoot off a bottle rocket.

Bud gives Ralph a Heath Bar. He doesn't like to spend his money on fireworks, but he does buy some Heath Bars to give out to people. Buddy gave his parents each a Heath Bar as he presented his father with a birthday card this morning. Bud likes to tease people, and he wants to tease his dad about being a "fire cracker," since he was born on July 4th. Bud knows that his father likes to tease, but he doesn't like to be teased by his son. John is rather stern with discipline, using his belt a few times to teach Bud lessons about good behavior. Nancy also disciplined him, but she had him cut his own switch from a tree for her to whip him with. If he didn't get a large enough one, she would send him back to get a different one.

Later that month, Bud rides over to Evanston again to see Dene. He finds out that the Pattersons are moving to a house in North Kansas City at the end of August. The Patterson house will be on East 21st Street in North Kansas City, and from his home it will be just a two mile ride on his bicycle instead of ten.

Mr. Patterson works at a railroad tank-car repair shop in North Kansas City industrial district. He has worked there for nine years. Now he is foreman of the shop, so other men climb into the tank cars to clean them. After they move to North Kansas City, Mrs. Patterson plans to work part time making clothing in the garment district of Kansas City, taking the bus to work. Bud and the girls play a game of Monopoly before Bud returns home. Bud wins the game.

The next time Bud comes home from his selling trip, he goes to see where the Patterson house is. It seems to him that the Pattersons must be rich, because they have a house with electricity, and even an indoor bathroom, which they did not have in their house at Evanston. They have an oil furnace, a telephone, an electric refrigerator, and an electric wringer-washing machine in the basement. *What a life!*

Before Bud's summer job with Mr. Jones is finished on August 15th, Bud saves up some money for a special gift, which he buys for Dene. He also buys himself a new light blue cardigan sweater, instead of getting a second-hand one.

The summer days at the last of August seem like a vacation to Bud, swimming and fishing in the boat again. He even finds time to use his fishing pole on the bank of the river.

When John comes home from work at the stadium, he swims with Bud to cool off before supper.

CHAPTER 7

Dating Years

Bud and Dene start their sophomore year at North Kansas City High School after Labor Day. After school one afternoon, Bud says, "Dene, I'd like to walk you home, and we can do our homework together."

"O.K." she replies. "Louise will be walking with us. She's a freshman this year, don't forget."

They enjoy the shade trees that line the twelve blocks from the high school to the Pattersons' house.

Winnie and Eldon arrive home about the same time from grade school. Dene's mother got home early, since work is slack. She is ironing clothes in the kitchen. She says, "Hello," and her children give her kisses as they arrive.

Bud says, "Hello, Mrs. Patterson, that looks like a hot job on a day like this."

She answers, "Yes, it is. Dene, you can get some pop out of the refrigerator if you want." They enjoy graham crackers and bottles of Coca-Cola while they study. When they finish, Bud walks the two miles home.

Friday of the same week, Dene tells Bud that her mother says she could invite him to come to Sunday dinner right after church on Sunday morning.

The Pattersons still drive to Antioch Community Church, where they attended when they lived in Evanston. Dene and Louise sing in the choir, and are in a young people's class of boys and girls for Sunday School. The Pattersons were members of Argentine Baptist Church in Kansas City, Kansas before they joined Antioch Community Church. At age 11 Dene became a Christian and was baptized in the Argentine Baptist Church.

Bud talks his mother into going to church with him at Harlem Baptist Church. Bud had persuaded her to attend a few other times. On this Sunday, she is saved. Baptism takes place down at the river after the service, like it was when Bud was saved. Bud is very happy about his mother being saved.

Bud rides his bike to Dene's house for dinner. They call their noon meal "dinner" and their evening meal "supper." That is different from what Buddy is used to. His family calls the noon meal lunch, and evening meal dinner. When he arrives at the Pattersons' house, he tells Dene and her family about his mother's decision and baptism. They rejoiced with him.

Dene and Louise put on fancy home-made aprons to help their mother prepare the food. Bud uses this time to read their Sunday funny paper while he waits. He somehow manages to slip from the living room to the dining room and pulls on Dene's apron string to untie it, and hurries away as she says, "Hey, you rascal!" She was discovering that Bud was quite a tease.

Bud thinks the dinner is elegant. There is a white table cloth on the dining room table. Guests who eat there could sign their names, which would be embroidered on the tablecloth later. They ate fried chicken, potato salad, slaw, corn, and hot rolls from the electric stove oven, plus cake and ice cream.

After dinner, all the young people play Monopoly. Louise wins the first game, and Bud wins the second one. It is time for a second piece of cake.

Then Bud and Dene sit on the front porch swing a little while. His arm is around her, and she does not object to it. Bud gives Dene a small package he has hidden in his pocket. She opens the package, and is very much surprised to find a very beautiful gold locket bracelet that has an expansion band.

"I saved money from the Hershey Candy job so I could get you this. I like you very much," says Bud.

"That's very sweet, but you shouldn't spend money on me," Dene says.

He answers, "I wanted to. Try it on."

"It fits perfectly," whispers Dene. "I'll put a picture of you and a picture of me in it." "Thanks so very much, I love it. I like you a lot, too."

They swing silently for a while, with her head on his shoulder. He gives her a kiss and goes home.

Dene goes inside to show everyone the beautiful bracelet etched with two hearts entwined, plus a pink flower with green leaves above and below the hearts, and a floral edging. The expansion band is the new popular, high-quality type of band. The bracelet becomes a treasure Dene wears often and keeps all her life as a special keepsake.

The Pattersons almost always go to the show on Saturday nights. The following Saturday, Bud meets them at the entrance to the local theater with his friend, Ralph. Bud has asked Louise at school if she would mind having a blind date with his friend, Ralph. When the boys meet the Pattersons at the Armour Theater that night, Bud introduces Ralph to Louise. He says, "This is my friend, Ralph. Could he sit with you in the show?"

"O.K.," she says. Bud and Ralph pay for the girls' tickets.

Bud says to Mr. Patterson, "Is it O.K. if we take the girls to the drugstore soda fountain before walking them home?" Mr. Patterson nods his approval.

Before they go into the theater, Mrs. Patterson calls Dene and Louise aside and whispers, "Remember, these boys don't have much money. Try to order the same thing they do, then that will give you a clue as to what they can afford." The three groups find seats in various rows.

Bud's birthday is coming up soon. Dene asks her parents about inviting him and Ralph to dinner close to Bud's birthday. Mrs. Patterson says, "That's a nice idea. We can have the dinner on the third Sunday in September. That's close to his birthday. Ask him at school."

"Oh, good. Ralph hasn't been here for dinner yet. It should be a lot of fun. What do you think we can give Bud for his birthday?"

"We'll think about it. The gift should just be from you, but the dinner will be from us," her mother answers.

Bud and Ralph ride their bikes up to the Pattersons' house the selected Sunday. As usual, when the girls are helping fix the dinner, Bud is getting sneaky, untying Louise's apron string, and then Dene's. The girls learn to watch out for him. He finds great delight in teasing people. This time, for Bud's sixteenth birthday, Mrs. Patterson makes his favorites: fried chicken, mashed potatoes with white gravy, corn and Waldorf salad, plus hot rolls again. After the dishes are cleared away, Dene brings the two-layer chocolate cake to the table with sixteen lighted candles on it.

She smiles and says, "Make a wish and blow the candles out."

Bud thinks a moment, and then blows them all out. Dene then hands him a package wrapped in blue paper with a red ribbon tied around it. Bud opens it, and finds a nice leather billfold. He is rather overwhelmed. On the verge of tears, he says, "Thank you, and thanks for the nice dinner."

Bud is asked to cut the first piece of cake, as is their tradition. Bud cuts the cake and gives the first piece to Dene. Mrs. Patterson cuts cake for everyone else, serving Bud first. Louise gets up and dips vanilla ice cream for everyone. After dessert, Chinese checkers is the first game played. Winnie and Eldon join in too. This is a rather new game in their area. They all try various ways to win. Dene wins the game. Later, they play one game of Monopoly. Bud wins.

"We just 'let him win' because it's his birthday," teases Ralph.

"Oh, sure," Bud says. "That's why I won."

Summer-like days in late September give John and Bud a few hot afternoons for swimming. They keep up their fishing as well. The water is a little high because of a series of thunder showers they had that week. It is a Friday. John is home from work and Bud is home from school. After a swim, John decides to dive off the A.S.B. bridge support like he has done several times before. Bud watches, and worries. His dad had been drinking earlier in the afternoon.

John makes a beautiful swan dive, but Bud hears a thud as his dad hits the water.

"What was that?" Bud yells.

John is just floating in the water, and then he begins to sink. Bud swims out to John, notices a cut on his head, and uses his life-saving techniques, learned at scouts, to rescue his dad. Bud notices a tree trunk submerged just under the water near the scene. The tree trunk was far enough below the surface that John hadn't seen it before diving. John is breathing, but the cut on his head is bleeding badly. Bud lays him on the bank and runs to the house for cloths he can use for bandages.

Nancy is cooking and asks, "What's the matter?"

"Dad dove in the river and hit his head on a log," cried Bud. He's cut badly. "I'll bandage it if you want to call a doctor."

Nancy says, "No, I'll bandage him, you run to the store and telephone for a doctor, if there is one in the office in North Kansas City this time of afternoon."

At the store, several people are there that Bud knows. Bud speaks to a Mr. Kaufman and says, "My dad had an accident. He dove off the bridge and hit his head on a log. Would you come in your car and take him to a doctor?"

"Oh, sure I will," Mr. Kaufman answers. Then he says to Billy Scott, the store clerk, "I'll give you fifty cents to deliver my groceries to my house when you get off of work. Will you do it.?"

Billy says, "I'm off work in a half hour. I'll take the groceries home for you."

"Thanks" says Mr. Kaufman as he hands Billy a half dollar, and the amount he owes for his groceries.

Bud rides with Mr. Kaufman to the place closest to their house. They both climb the levy and find Nancy hovering over John, where she has covered him up to keep him warm. His head is bandaged and he is breathing, but his eyes are closed and he is unresponsive. Nancy and Bud are quite worried. The three of them wrap John in a blanket, and together, carry him up across the levy. As they come down, they see Happy in his yard. Happy hurries to help them.

"What happened?" he asks.

Bud is crying now, but he answers, "He dove in the river and hit his head on a log. We're going to take him to a doctor."

"You'd best take him directly to the General Hospital in Kansas City. That's not very far and he looks pretty bad," says Happy.

"That's what we will do, if that's alright with you, Mr. Kaufman," Nancy says. They lay John down in the back seat and the three of them squeeze into the front seat. Nancy keeps an eye on John as they drive.

"General Hospital takes patients even if they can't pay," Mr. Kaufman says.

When they arrive at the hospital, John is examined and declared to be in a coma.

"When will he likely come out of the coma?" Nancy asks.

"That's a question no one can answer at this time," the doctor says. They move him up to a room that has another patient in it.

Nancy tells Mr. Kaufman, "You've been a great friend. Now I know why the children in the neighborhood call you and your wife Pa and Ma Kaufman. Thank you very much. We'll take a bus home to Harlem later tonight. Would you mind feeding Bear for us? I had started cooking some potatoes when this accident happened. I did get the fire turned off. After the fire we had recently, I've been extra careful to turn the stove off when interrupted. Thanks again."

Nancy and Bud watch the nurses take care of John. They seem to be doing a good job. They ask if Nancy and Bud are hungry.

Nancy says, "We didn't have supper yet. But we'll get something when we get home." The nurse leaves and comes back with two ham and cheese sandwiches, and two pints of milk.

She says, "Your husband won't be able to eat tonight, so you can eat these. You need to keep up your strength."

Nancy and Bud thank her. They are quite grateful for the food and the kind care John is getting.

By 10:00 p.m., Nancy says to Bud, "We can't help your daddy any more tonight. Maybe he will be awake tomorrow. We'll come back by bus and see how he is."

They both kiss John and leave. There are many tears that night from both of them, and some drinking by Nancy. But eventually they sleep, waking rather late the next morning.

After a breakfast of cereal and toast, Nancy and Bud walk up to the bus stop near the A.S.B. Bridge and catch a bus. They are silent during the ride. Both are having trouble absorbing the enormity of the situation they are in.

While they are in the hospital, Bud looks up his grandpa's telephone number and calls him from a pay phone in the lobby of the hospital. Minerva answers and finds out Bud wants to talk to Julius. Grandpa hurries to the phone.

Bud says, "Hello Grandpa, this is Bud."

"Why, Hello, Bud," grandpa says. "Is there something wrong?"

Bud answers, "Mother and I want you to know that daddy has had an accident. He dove off the bridge support and hit his head on a log. He has a bad cut on his head, and he is in a coma. The doctor does not know how long he will be in a coma. He is at General Hospital."

Grandpa inquires, "When would be a good time for me to visit John, do you think?"

Bud suggests, "Maybe tomorrow, while Mother and I are at church. I have the school's cello home, and I'm supposed to play it with the pianist as the people sing hymns at church tomorrow."

Grandpa says, "Thanks for calling me. I'll go see him tomorrow morning, for sure. Are you doing alright, Bud?"

"Sure, I'm alright, Grandpa. I'm just sad about daddy's accident," he answers.

After Nancy and Bud get back home, Bud decides there is enough daylight that he could take the boat and go up the Kaw River and seine a load of fish. First he goes to ask Ralph to go with him. It would be hard for one person. Ralph gladly accepts the invitation. He has time before going to deliver telegrams.

Bud thinks that people will be coming to buy fish both that night and Sunday night. Bud really feels like a "Fisher Boy" now. It is up to him, and him alone, to keep food on the table. At least it isn't getting cold yet, so they don't need to buy coal.

Grandpa Julius goes to the hospital to see his son, John, but he becomes quite depressed about it. He hadn't seen John very much after he and his family moved to the river area. John was so busy fishing and working for the W.P.A. that he had very little time to go anywhere. Julius goes to see John every Sunday after that. Nancy and Bud go to see him every Saturday. Bud calls the hospital every day to find out if John is out of the coma. There isn't much they can do for him. Bud and Ralph fish every day, and sell and clean the fish like John had done. Bud gives Ralph some of the fish for helping him.

It normally doesn't get really cold until the first part of December. Bud buys some coal in November. He chops down several small trees to use for kindling, and one tree a little bigger to use as firewood instead of coal.

There is plenty for him to do at home, so Bud doesn't go to the Pattersons' after school. He does go once in a while on Sunday after church. The Pattersons are very sympathetic about his situation, but they don't know what they can do, except invite him to a good meal whenever he can come.

Bud and Ralph go to the Pattersons for Thanksgiving dinner. Mrs. Patterson asks Bud to bring his mother to dinner, but she goes to eat with the Kaufmans.

Mrs. Patterson serves goose, and a wide variety of other dishes, as always. She is an excellent cook. She also has made some of her home-made, raised, glazed donuts, plus pumpkin pie and mincemeat pie. The young people play games as usual. These occasions will be long remembered by all the young people.

On December 7th of that year, 1941, Nancy and Bud are listening to the radio when the announcer says, "News Flash! Japan has just bombed Pearl Harbor on the island of Oahu, Hawaii. President Roosevelt will speak about the matter shortly."

The Pattersons also hear the announcement. People all over the country are shocked. When President Roosevelt speaks he declares that:

"The United States is now at war with Japan. This day shall go down in infamy!" People are stunned. They talk about it all the time and many young men and women sign up to enter the various branches of service, knowing they will be going to war.

The war is on Bud's mind now. He is too young to sign up for service, but he wants to go. He is experiencing grief from the war situation, as well as grief from the fact that his dad is still in a coma.

The hospital has been given the phone number of the Harlem Store. Someone there will take them a message if it is important. On December 22, the hospital calls. Billy Scott answers.

"Yes," he says, "I can take a message to Nancy Weideman."

The nurse on the phone says, "Tell Mrs. Weideman that her husband just passed away. She will need to make arrangements for him today and let us know where to send him." Billy restrains himself from crying out on the phone. He dearly loves the Weideman family.

The owner lets Billy go long enough to carry the message to them. Billy knocks on the door. Bud is out of school for the Christmas holidays. He answers the door.

"Come in," Bud invites.

"Alright, for just a few minutes. I have a phone message for you and your mother."

Nancy comes through the living room door from the kitchen and asks, "What is it?"

"The hospital called. They tell me that John passed away this morning. I am very sorry. They want you to go to the hospital and make arrangements to take him some place."

Nancy breaks into tears and Bud puts his arms around her and lets her cry on his shoulder. He is crying too. They loved John very much. They had hoped he would come out of his coma, but knew it was unlikely.

"Sorry, I have to leave," Billy says, "but let me know if I can do something to help you."

Nancy and Bud gain control of their emotions after awhile, and get ready to go to the hospital for one last time. On the bus they talk about what they can do. They don't have money for a funeral.

At the hospital, a chaplain talks to them.

He says, "We understand that John did not have insurance, and you have no way to pay for a funeral. There is a cemetery just across the Kansas River in Kansas City, Kansas where people can be buried if they have no money for burial. Would you like for us to send him there and have a grave-side ceremony for him? You can ask any pastor you want to hold the grave-side service."

Nancy thinks about the situation a few minutes before answering him. She is so sad that it is hard to talk at all.

"It is so near Christmas, I wonder when we could have the funeral?" she asks.

The chaplain suggests, "The hospital could have him prepared for burial, and hold him until the day after Christmas. That would let you have a service December. 26th."

"I'll talk to our pastor and see if he can do it then," Nancy says. "We will call you later today and let you know."

On their walk home from the bus station to Harlem they stop at the parsonage. When the pastor opens the door Nancy begins crying as she tells him why she came. The pastor is very kind.

He says, "I'm so sorry. I'll be glad to do the service. My wife and I will take you and Bud with us to the funeral." Since he has a phone and they don't, he offers to make the phone call to the chaplain at the hospital and tell him what they have decided.

The pastor muses, "How old was he?"

Nancy answers, "He just turned 39 on July 4th."

"Such a sad thing," the pastor says.

Bud takes his mother on home. He knows he has two other people to call. He goes back to the Harlem store to use their pay phone. First he calls his grandpa. Minerva answers the phone and calls Julius.

Julius says cheerfully, "Hello, Fisher Boy. How are you today? Bud has a hard time telling Grandpa that his son is dead. Grandpa doesn't stay on the phone long. He is very sad. Bud tells him about the arrangements.

Next, Bud calls the Pattersons.

Dene answers cheerfully, "Hello, how is your dad doing now?"

Bud has to tell her, "He passed away this morning."

Dene softly speaks, "I'm so very sorry. Are you and your mother doing O.K.?"

Bud is pretty quiet now, but manages, "We're making plans for a grave-side service on the day after Christmas. Our pastor and his wife will take us there. It's in Kansas City, Kansas."

Dene speaks, "I'd like to go with you to the funeral."

But Bud is firm, "No, I'd rather you didn't go. You can't do anything, really, and it will be short."

"Will you and Ralph come for dinner on Christmas? Your mother could come too, if she wants to."

"Yes, Ralph and I will come, but I'll let you know if my mother wants to come," Bud answers.

When Dene's parents hear about John's death Mrs. Patterson tells Dene, "Go to the grocery store to buy a nice box of Christmas chocolates for Bud's mother. She may come, and even if she doesn't, we can send it to her."

Christmas Day is bright after an inch of snow falls on Christmas Eve. The Pattersons go to a Christmas Program at the Antioch Community Church on Christmas Eve, and Santa comes while they are gone. It seems that Mrs. Patterson is always rather late getting out to the car while the family waits for her to "finish getting ready." This is a custom from the time the children were young— even when they were members of the Argentine Baptist Church in Kansas City, Kansas, while they lived in Argentine, and then Armourdale. When they returned home from the program, they saw their gifts, not wrapped, but sitting under the fir tree. Now that the children are older, they still open their gifts after the Christmas program, but the gifts are wrapped. The Pattersons typically decorate the tree ahead of time with strings of popcorn, cranberry chains, red and green chains the children make from construction paper, tinsel icicles, and a few electric lights.

On this bright Christmas Day guests are coming. Bud and Ralph arrive mid-morning. Bud and his mother were both invited to dinner at the home of Pa and Ma Kaufman, so Nancy goes there by herself. The Weidemans are becoming like family to the Kaufmans.

The girls watch their apron strings. Bud's teasing isn't quite as prominent as usual. He is rather subdued, understandably. Before dinner Bud and Dene exchange gifts; and so do Ralph and Louise. Bud gives Dene a set of Evening in Paris perfume, bath powder in a round box, and a fancy bar of soap. The perfume comes in a dark royal blue color—a tall thin bottle with a tassel on the cap. Dene likes it very much. Bud and Ralph each get a scarf and ear muffs from the girls. What a surprise, Louise gets the same thing Dene does.

For this turkey dinner, one special dish is Waldorf salad, which is always served at Christmas, and sometimes Thanksgiving, too. This time there is dressing and cranberry sauce to go with the turkey, along with traditional Christmas dishes and home-made sugar cookies decorated with colored icing.

After dinner Mr. Patterson treats everyone to a movie at their usual movie house, the Armour Theater in North Kansas City. There is a Christmas movie showing and a cute cartoon. Bud seems to cheer up a little.

Bud is busy trying to catch enough fish for their customers, and keeping enough wood for their heating stove, plus kerosene for their stove and lamps. He works what time he can at the hamburger stand again.

In February, Bud wants to do something different for entertainment. He asks Dene to go skating with him. They take the bus and go to the El Torium Skating Rink in Kansas City. They both skate pretty well. Bud tries skating backwards and, after a few tries, figures out how to do it and stay upright. Dene tries it, and eventually is able to skate backwards, too. They skate together part of the time and separate part of the time. The last skate of the evening is "Partners Only" for a "Moonlight Waltz." The lights dim a little, turning blue, green, and light red in streaks overhead. The skaters enjoy keeping time to the waltz music, with arms around the waist and hands held in front. It is a wonderful time to remember. Dene is really pleased to be dating an Eagle Scout who is a Christian and is such a good-looking guy to have fun with.

Nancy decides that she should look for a job. She watches help wanted ads in the newspaper and interviews for some that don't pan out. Finally, near the end of February, she is hired for a job as a maid in a hotel in Kansas City. She is given a room to live in, and a wage that will keep her going.

Bud decides that he needs to leave the river area too. Being a Fisher Boy will have to wait until later in his life.

"I have caught rather large fish, but there must be more to life than just reeling in big fish," he thinks to himself.

In March, Bud moves to a basement room for rent in North Kansas City. By working at the hamburger stand he eats cheaply and has enough for the rent, and a little for fun times, too. It is close enough to Dene that they can walk to school together. Bud rides his bike to work to save bus fare.

Each weekend he and Ralph eat Sunday dinner at the Pattersons. Bud starts going to Antioch Church with the Pattersons. He doesn't get to play his cello for services, but he and Dene are in a mixed Sunday School class together. The class has monthly parties. The church has outdoor pageants in the summer, telling Bible stories on a stage built under the trees on the church lot. Dene and her sisters take part in the pageants. Dene drops out of choir so she can sit with Bud in church.

Bud seems to be healing somewhat from the hurt of his father's death. He and Dene skate about every three weeks, and go to the show on Saturdays.

Playing in the orchestra during graduation that year is bitter sweet. Bud is thinking he will enter military service as soon as he can. He really loves playing the cello, but he needs a more stable life, somehow.

By June first, Ralph tells Bud that there is an opening for another person to deliver telegrams at Postal Telegraph where he works. Bud applies and gets the job, a full-time day job for the summer, so he gives up his hamburger stand job.

Bud and Dene are together a lot. When swinging on the Patterson's front porch, there are more kisses, and Bud tells Dene that he is in love with her. Dene feels the same about him, but doesn't say so at first. She talks to her mother about it.

Her mother says, "If you really feel that way too, you can tell him, but just help him to not get too entangled. You are both too young to get serious about each other."

Bud tells Dene that he really wants to make love to her. He asks permission.

She says, "No, we can't do that. I love you too, but that's not right. That's what marriage is for. So no, we can't do that." He asks her quite a few times. The answer is always "No."

On July 13th, 1942, Bud enlists in the Marine Corps. He tells Dene, "I just joined the Marines so we can be apart for awhile. We're getting too close and the only way I can handle it is to leave for awhile. I want you to have my Eagle Scout pin."

Dene takes the pin and says, "I really love you, but you are right. We are getting too close. Also, we haven't really dated any other people to compare each other with."

Then Bud shows her a ring with a small stone, which he says is for being engaged to be engaged.

"But," he says, "we will be apart for a long time, and if either one of us wants to go out with other people we can do it. Let's tell each other in letters when we go out with someone else. Is that alright with you?"

Dene says, "Yes, that's alright. The way I feel I will always love you. But in case either of us changes our minds, we can figure things out at that time."

"Then you accept the ring that way?" he asks.

"Yes. I hate to see you go, but lots of guys are going now. Be careful. I'm proud to have your Eagle Scout pin as well as the ring. We will write often, won't we?"

"Of course. You can write me every day if you want to," he laughs. "I'll send you my address when I get to Camp Pendleton in California."

"I thought you were too young to sign up. How did you do it?"

"I told them I was 17. I will be 17 in two months. My mother had to sign to say I am seventeen. She told them my birth certificate burned up in the fire we had awhile back. She thought it was a good idea for me to go on into the service. It pays more than I can make here. We can't have a home together by the river anymore."

When the day comes for Bud to leave, Mr. Patterson and Dene take him to the train station in Kansas City to meet the people he is going with. Dene gives him a Bible and they exchange pictures of each other before they part with a kiss, the first kiss they are not trying to hide from her parents. Bud puts on a brave face, but has tears inside, and Dene does too.

CHAPTER 8

Marine Years and Marriage

Dene's first communication from Fisher Boy in California is a picture postcard with his address, and little else. The Marine recruits are kept pretty busy after they arrive at Camp Pendleton. It feels good to have all new clothes, which he never had before. Meals are regular and plentiful. Bud starts getting acquainted with fellow Marines.

Basic training is rigorous, to say the least. It has to be in order to toughen up the fellows so they will have a chance of coming through the war successfully. Bud likes the shooting at the rifle course. He becomes a sharp shooter. Pistols are taught also. Shooting and cleaning the weapons is important.

Bud gets a week-end pass before being shipped over seas. One of his buddies had a sister that lives in San Diego. He asks Bud if he would like to have a date with her. Bud decides he can rent a car and take the girl skating. He is missing skating sessions with Dene. Besides, he thinks it might be a long time before he will have a chance to have any fun again. Bud writes and tells Dene about the date. She is jealous, but puts that aside because of what they promised each other.

In Boy Scouts, Bud learned International Morse Code, so he is given the opportunity to become a radio operator who sends messages to other troops by Morse Code. In service they use the American Morse Code. Just a few of the letters are different from International. He learns the

65

difference in his training. Bud's main job is being a radio operator. He carries an SCR 135 radio. He tries to hide behind it to dodge bullets.

Bud is sent to Auckland, New Zealand to finish his training. He starts in the Headquarters Co., 9th Marine Regiment, 3rd Marine Division.

The first big battle Bud faces is at Guadalcanal. Another difficult battle is at Bougainville. There he uses a sub-machine gun that shoots 45-caliber bullets. Sometimes Bud used a 45 caliber pistol or a rifle. At Bougainville the 9th Marine Regiment is broken up. Bud is now in the 4th Marine Regiment.

The next big battle takes place at Guam. Bud is in the 4th Marine Regiment, Headquarters Co., 1st Provisional Brigade. The 4th Marine Regiment is made up of Radar Battalions. President Roosevelt's son is in charge of one of them. The 4th Marines is an elite group. Bud is in one of the elite groups. They use Navaho Indians to pass messages in the Navaho language. The Indians are called Navaho Talkers. The Japanese never do break their Navaho language code. One of the Navaho Talkers is assigned to Bud. His name is Watonka Hunter. Watonka is three years older than Bud, and he seems to remember knowing Bud when he was a little boy. He mentions it to Bud. Bud remembers his mother and father talking about a family of Navaho Indians that were their friends, helping Bud to get well when he had polio.

"Could you be the same Watonka that was the oldest son of Morning Star and Chief Brave Hunter?" Bud asks.

Watonka answers, "Those are my parents."

Bud and Watonka are extremely excited to be together after all these years. Each of them tells about their family from the time they had seen each other as little children. What a wonderful surprise. They each feel like they have a family member with them. Watonka is sad to hear about Bud's father's accident and death.

During the time that Bud is out fighting the war, Dene finishes high school. When it is nearing time for the senior prom Dene decides she wants a date for the prom. So, she talks to one of her girl friends who has a boy cousin in their class. He is a pretty nice fellow. She gets her girl friend to talk the fellow into asking her to the prom. The catch in his mind is that he knows Bud and Dene are an item. He doesn't want to take Bud's girl out while he is in service. But Dene explains to him about the agreement between her and Bud.

After hearing that, he is happy to take Dene to the prom. He gives her a rose corsage and they enjoy the evening. He uses his parents' car to take Dene to the prom.

Dene writes to tell Bud about the prom. Every few months Dene bakes cookies and sends them to Bud. She pops corn to put in with the cookies in an attempt to keep the cookies from breaking up. Dene also sends other small items. Bud likes the cookies better than anything he can think of for her to send him. She always sends them on Christmas and birthdays along with whatever gift she can think of to send.

The Patterson girls start baby-sitting for couples during the evenings. Dene takes a summer job as produce worker at a local grocery store. Another summer she works in a department store in Kansas City.

When she graduates from high school, Dene goes to William Jewell Baptist College in Liberty for two years while Bud is still in the service. She majors in psychology, but the classes she enjoys most are taught by Dr. H.I. Hester - Old Testament History, and the next year New Testament History. Dene works in the dining room of the dormitory to pay for her room and board. During the summer between her freshman and sophomore years of college, Dene works as a secretary at Standard Steel Corporation in the North Kansas City industrial district. Dene took secretarial courses in high school. She is a very fast typist, and takes shorthand at 100 words a minute.

During Christmas vacation Dene and her friend Amy work at the Kansas City Post Office sorting mail. Amy is from California, so the Pattersons invite her to spend the two holiday weeks with them so both girls can work at the Post Office.

Many of the students at William Jewell feel that God has called them to be missionaries. Dene doesn't feel that kind of call from God, but she really wants God to give her some kind of special call. She feels that God is telling her to marry a Christian man and raise a very good Christian family.

The Pattersons plant a little "Victory Garden" in their back yard, so named to show support for the troops. Their son Eldon becomes an Eagle Scout, following in the steps of Bud. Ralph tries to enlist in the Army, but has a punctured ear drum, so he is labeled 4-F, meaning they won't take him in the Army. While Bud is away, Ralph and Louise decide to get married. They ask the preacher to marry them without any frills. It is war time, after all.

Winnie is in the high school orchestra, just as her two sisters had been. She is also a cheer leader for the football team. She wears a cute purple and gold outfit.

Winnie later meets a young man named Archie who is in the Navy. After he finishes his tour of duty, they are married.

There is a popular song going around during the war called *"Three Little Sisters."* The Patterson sisters say it fits them, and they sing it a lot. The three little sisters in the song have boyfriends in the Army, Navy and the Marines. The sisters stay home and read their magazines and remain true to their service boyfriends. That is the way the Patterson girls felt.

Bud fights on many islands in the Pacific, in small and big battles. He is in another big battle on Okinawa. After that, his unit is nearing Japan's main island, ready to fight there, when Japan surrenders - August 14, 1945. Instead of entering Japan to fight, the Marines become Tokyo Bay Occupation Force (TF-31). They participate in the initial landing and occupation of the Tokyo Bay Area, and the capture of Hijms Nagato, which act symbolizes the unconditional and complete surrender of the Japanese Navy, August 30, 1945. Bud's certificate is signed by military officials, including Brigadier General United States Marine Corps, Commander Fleet Landing Force, Commanding Officer Captain, Fourth Marine Regiment, and Rear Admiral, United States Navy Commander Tokyo Bay Occupation Force.

What a relief to Bud, his mother and grandparents, and the Pattersons, that he makes it through all that tough fighting.

"God had his hand on Bud, saving him for some special purpose," Dene thought.

While Bud is in Japan he takes the opportunity to study for, and pass, his GED, to graduate from High School.

That Christmas, 1945, Bud is finally given a leave to come home for 30 days. He stays with a friend whose family lives near Dene's. He goes to the Pattersons for Christmas Eve and again Christmas Day.

On Christmas Eve, Bud and Dene have a few minutes alone in the living room. Bud takes a ring box from his pocket and says, "Dene, I love you very much. I hope you still love me. I want to marry you."

Dene says, "I really do love you. I think about you all the time. Yes, I want to marry you, too."

Bud puts the ring on her finger and kisses her. They don't care that some members of the family are in the dining room watching now. She gets up and proudly shows the family and Amy her engagement ring.

A little later Bud and Dene discuss when they should get married. Bud signed up in the Marines for four years, so he still has to stay in the service until July of 1946. Dene says she would like to get married right away so she can go with him as he serves the last few months. But Bud tells her that housing for married service men is very poor, and he thinks they should plan a wedding for the summertime.

They decide to set the date for August, 1946, about a month after he is discharged from service. That way Dene can finish her current year of college. They have an especially happy Christmas Day.

During the years that Bud is in service, he sends money to Mr. Patterson and asks him to put it in the bank for him so he can buy a car when he gets out of service. He also has an allotment sent to his mother, of course. He has very little he can spend money on while he is in service in all those battles. Bud waits until he gets discharged to get the money from Mr. Patterson.

During the last few months of college Dene discusses plans for her wedding with Amy and Dene's roommate, Esther, who is from New Jersey. Dene saved money from her summer jobs so she could buy her own wedding gown.

Shortly before school is out that spring, both girl friends go home with Dene for the weekend. They go with her to pick out her wedding gown. It is made of lace over satin with a long train. She has a shoe ration stamp that she uses to buy her white leather two-inch high heels to go with the wedding dress.

One of the ladies at Antioch Church offers to let Dene use her veil. The veil will be something borrowed. Every bride is supposed to have "something old, something new, something borrowed and something blue." Dene buys a pair of blue garters. She has a lacey handkerchief given to her previously by her grandmother. That is the old item. Of course, her clothes are new. Now, all the special items are taken care of.

Dene and Bud are both 20 years old when Bud receives an honorable discharge from the Marine Corps on July 12, 1946. He returns by train to Kansas City. Dene and her mother and father go to pick him up at the Union Station in Kansas City. He stays with the friend he boarded with at Christmas time.

Bud and Dene are members of a Sunday School class for young couples. They throw a party for Bud and Dene, and present them with gifts.

The class members each use a page in a large scrap book to put pictures and messages, cut out from magazines, predicting how they think their coming life together will be. Most are funny and cartoon-like. The class also volunteers to decorate the stage of the church with their home-grown flowers and ferns, to make a beautiful background for the candelabras.

Bud buys a car shortly before the wedding. He and Dene drive to William Jewell in Liberty. Bud enrolls, using the G.I. Bill provided to veterans of the war for continuing their education. They rent a furnished house near the college, which consists of one room and one bathroom.

Just before the wedding date, Bud's mother goes to the Pattersons' house by bus and brings the young couple a beautiful bowl as a wedding gift.

She says, "Every bride needs a fancy bowl."

Dene hugs her and says, "I love it. Thank you very much."

Mrs. Patterson asks her to stay for dinner that night, but she says she has to get back to work. She also says she won't be able to go to the wedding.

The evening before the wedding, Bud and Dene go to the drugstore for old time's sake, like they did while dating. Then they drive to Dene's home and park. Bud reminds Dene of the times he had asked her to let him make love to her. She remembers, alright.

Bud says to her, "You know, if you had given in to me, I never would have married you. I really wanted you to be pure for our wedding, but I really desired you, also. I'm really glad you didn't give in."

They kiss good-night and she goes inside. Dene's father is in the living room. He is surprised to see her come in at 10:00 p.m.

She tells him, "We just said what we needed to say to each other. Tomorrow will be a big day. People getting married are not supposed to see each other before the wedding, but we plan to go with you and mother to the Sunday morning breakfast that your Sunday School Class has once a month. We're not superstitious."

At 7:30 p.m. that Sunday evening in August, 1946, Reverend Burkhart reads the double-ring ceremony at the Antioch Community Church.

The bride wears a gown of white lace with a long train, fashioned with a sweetheart neckline, and long sleeves ending in a point. A finger-tip veil falls from her lacey white cap. She carries a bouquet of white gladioli. Her sister Winnie is maid of honor. Winnie's dress is made of pink chiffon, and she carries yellow gladioli.

The bride's young cousin, Barbara, is the flower girl. A young boy from the church named Monty serves as the ring-bearer. Before the ceremony, a lady from the church sings the songs "Because" and "I Love You Truly." Just before the benediction, "The Lord's Prayer" is sung. The bride's sister Louise is pianist for the occasion.

A friend of the groom, James Spencer, is best man for Corporal Warren Lee Weideman, who wears his Marine Corps dress blue uniform.

Grandpa and Grandma Weideman come to the wedding. Bud is very glad for the chance to introduce Dene and her family to his grandparents. They had not met before.

After the wedding, a reception is held in the basement of the church following the ceremony. The three-tiered wedding cake and punch are served to the guests. The bride and groom open many nice gifts. Bud's grandparents give them a small electric washing machine that holds as much as one sheet.

Dene is quite surprised and says, "I'm so happy about that! It's a lot easier to use than going to a Laundromat."

Dene's parents give them a two-burner hot-plate and a toaster oven. Her sisters and brother give them an electric iron and an ironing board.

After the wedding, the bride and groom find their car decorated with crepe-paper streamers, tin cans tied to the back bumper, and "Just Married" written on the back window with shaving cream. They run out through a barrage of rice, jump into the car, and head for their little rented house in Liberty, Missouri. Dene's parents will bring the wedding gifts on another day.

Bud and Dene are inside their house about ten minutes, when they hear numerous cars drive up, honking their horns. The occupants of the cars flood into the tiny house and attempt to make themselves at home. The gang, (otherwise known as their Sunday school classmates), has brought leftover cake from the reception, and they decide to stay and talk for quite a long time. Finally, someone has pity on the bride and groom and ushers everyone out the door.

Finally, the couple is alone. Dene sits on the edge of the bed, and Bud unbuttons all those satin-covered buttons down the back of her dress. He rather enjoys that, even though it takes quite awhile. The lights go out and she lies down in his out-stretched arms.

The next morning they both have to be on "The Hill" as the college campus is called. Bud has an 8:00 class and Dene is working at the Alumni Office as a secretary. It is a good thing they had an alarm clock. The couple had brought a few food items and their clothes into the house before the wedding. They each eat a bowl of cereal, and are out the door to start their life as Mr. and Mrs. Weideman.

Bud enjoys the classes. He meets some other students who invite him to their Chess Club. One of Bud's buddies in service played chess with him. The friend had a small set he carried in his backpack. Dene joins him at the

Chess Club meeting, and watches them play. She has learned the game from Bud, but isn't very good at it. Before the semester is over, Bud is voted in as President of the Chess Club, because he wins most of the games.

On days when Bud does not have afternoon classes, he goes to a pool hall and plays a few games for recreation. He watches some good players and learns the "bank shots" and other little tricks from advanced competitors. Bud works hard at everything he tries, and demonstrates skill quickly.

Shortly after Bud and Dene are married, Dene's sister, Winnie, and her boyfriend from the Navy, Archie, are married. They live north of North Kansas City, but a few years later buy a house in Kansas City. Louise and Ralph have a son, Ralph Lee.

At Christmas vacation time, Dene thinks she is pregnant. While they are in North Kansas City for the holidays, she goes to a doctor, who confirms her pregnancy, with a due date around August 15th. This makes Bud decide to switch from college to full-time work. He comes up with the idea of using his car as a taxi. The young couple is invited to move in with the Patterson family so Dene can be near their family doctor and Bud can get his taxi cab company started.

Dene does not work. Instead, she makes baby clothes and keeps up with Bud's busy schedule as taxi driver and owner of a business, as other people with cars join his group of taxis.

On March 27, 1947 Bud receives a call from the owner of the hotel where his mother works. He tells Bud that Nancy has passed away in her sleep from an apparent heart attack. Bud, Dene and her parents attend a graveside service for her, just like Bud and Nancy had done for his father, John. He is able to obtain a photo album from the few things Nancy had at the hotel. This is a very sad time for Bud and Dene. Nancy had been looking forward to becoming a grandmother, and Dene had hoped to get better acquainted with her new mother-in-law.

Bud plans to get off work and take Dene to the movies to celebrate their first wedding anniversary in August. Before their set time to leave, while Bud is still out driving, Dene's water breaks. Her parents call the taxi office phone, which is in the home of one of the taxi drivers, whose wife takes the calls. They tell her to have Bud come home as soon as possible to take Dene to the hospital. Bud is on a long run. Dene's parents decide to go ahead and take her to the hospital. Eldon will be alright home alone.

The cost of the hospital stay for a birth and week's stay in Research Hospital, $50.00, has to be paid before Dene can be admitted. Mr. Patterson pays it. Dene is taken to a delivery room. Bud arrives at the hospital before the baby is born. He gets to say a few words of encouragement to Dene, and give her a kiss. Then he has to go with her parents to the waiting room. Fathers are not allowed to be in the delivery room. While they wait, Bud learns about the $50.00 being already paid by Mr. Patterson. Bud thanks him and pays the money to him. The doctor charges another $50.00, but he waits awhile for his money.

It is 12:45 a.m. the next morning that Esther Louise is born.

She misses their first anniversary by forty-five minutes. This is an anniversary they will never forget.

Dene was under a mild sedation during the birth, and barely saw the baby in the delivery room. She asks the doctor whether it is a boy or girl.

The nurse answers, "She's a healthy baby girl weighing 7 pounds and 3 ounces and is twenty and one-half inches long."

Bud gets to see Dene shortly after the baby is delivered.

"Are you O. K., honey?" Bud asks.

"Yes," she says, "I'm just tired. You know, when you smile like you are smiling now *your blue eyes just twinkle.*"

"Well, I'm happy that you had the baby and that you are both alright. You wanted to name a girl Esther Louise, didn't you?"

"Yes," Dene says. Bud kisses her and goes with the Pattersons to the nursery window to look at the baby.

"Esther Louise really is cute, isn't she?" Bud asks Dene's mother.

"Of course she is," Mrs. Patterson says. "She's got your curly hair."

"The nurse made a curl in that blond hair on the top of her head. Dene always had to get permanents to make her hair curly. She will have fun taking care of Esther's curly hair." Mrs. Patterson continues.

They return to Dene's room and they all talk about how cute the baby looks. Just then, a nurse from the nursery brings the baby into the room so Dene can see her all cleaned up with her hair curled. The baby lies in her arms as the nurse rolls the top of the bed up a little for Dene to hold the baby a few minutes.

Dene says, "Honey, she has blond curly hair like you had in your early pictures. She sure is cute."

After a few minutes, the nurse takes the baby back to the nursery. Bud and her parents kiss Dene and they go home to let her sleep, and get some sleep themselves.

The next day Bud calls his grandparents to tell them about the baby girl. They are thrilled at the news. When Esther is a month old, Great Grandpa and Great Grandma Weideman come to visit at the Pattersons' house. They bring a baby spoon and fork for Esther. Bud loves watching his grandpa hold Esther. He remembers how happy his grandpa was playing with him as a little boy.

"Grandpa," Bud says, "won't it be fun when you can let Esther ride the horse on your foot like I used to do."

Grandpa is overwhelmed with happiness, and says, "When she gets old enough, I hope to be able to do that."

Dene's mother insists they stay for supper. They have pork chops and mashed potatoes. Then the grandparents return home in their truck.

CHAPTER 9

Early Married Years

In September Bud's car is wrecked by one of the taxi drivers. Collision insurance is all he has on the car, so the totaled vehicle ends Bud's occupation as taxi driver. The driver was lucky not to be hurt.

Bud decides he will go to a trade school in Kansas City. He learns that in Rail Road School they teach Morse code, which is something he already knows. Bud enrolls in Railroad School. He also signs up in the Marine Reserves in order to have a monthly check while he goes to school. Bud shows his birth certificate in order to correct his age on his Marine records.

Bud, Dene and their baby girl, move close to his school, located on 12th Street in Kansas City. An old hotel, the Coats House, rents rooms by the week or month, and accommodates their needs for the time being. Because of her colic, the baby cries almost every night until she is three months old. The manager of Coats House tells Bud that he and his family are disturbing the other residents, and that they will have to move.

Bud hears from friends about a third-floor apartment for rent at 1225 Penn, just a half block from Twelfth Street. There is a bedroom and a large kitchen, both furnished, in a multi-family residence. Bud buys Dene a rocking chair to use for the baby, and a baby bed. The use of electrical appliances is frowned upon. It costs another fifty cents a week for every electrical appliance they have. The apartment rents for $8.00 a week, plus

fifty cents for their radio. The washing machine given to
them by Bud's grandparents is not allowed on the third
floor. The landlord expects people to use the Laundromat
around the corner. The only kitchen-type sink is in the
hall, shared by them and three other apartments. The
bathroom is also shared by the four apartments. With the
service men coming back home and starting families,
apartments are difficult to find. They are glad to have one
close to where Bud's school is.

The apartment is on Quality Hill, on the west side of
Kansas City. It overlooks the area of the Missouri River
where Bud and his parents lived. Things are very
different, but still quite difficult for Bud and his new little
family.

There is an ice box in their apartment that holds up to
50 pounds of ice to keep food cold. There is a pan under
it to collect water as the ice melts. The ice company drives
down the street every week day. They give people cards to
put in their window to show what size of ice block the
customer wants. The size of ice blocks ranges from 25 to
100 pounds. The delivery man uses ice tongs and carries
the ice up the stairs to the person's apartment. He puts a
gunnysack on his shoulder and holds the ice against it to
carry it up all those steps.

Dene applies for work, and is hired as typist in the
Montgomery Ward Mail Order House on the east side of
Kansas City. She finds a baby-sitter just a half block
away from their apartment. She leaves the baby with Mrs.
Perkins, who tells funny stories about Esther's daily
activities. Mrs. Perkins recalls an incident where a crate
of eggs was delivered to their house, and she set the
carton on the floor as she went to get money to pay for the
eggs. When she comes back to the door, she notices
Esther dropping one egg after another on the floor. Mrs.
Perkins talks sternly to Esther, and puts her in a play
pen, while she cleans up the mess. When she tells Dene
about it, she doesn't let Esther see the smile on her face.
She knows she should have put Esther in her play pen
before going out of the room.

The year that Esther is born, all three Patterson sisters have a daughter three months apart. Winnie's is first, named Sandra, then Dene's daughter, Esther, and then Louise's daughter, Judy--*three little cousins, from three sisters.*

Esther is still a toddler when Dene discovers she is pregnant again, with a due date of December 25, 1949.

Bud finishes his Rail Road School training. He applies for a job with Missouri Pacific Railroad at their Kansas City office, and is hired. His first assignment is to give a vacation to the station agent at Olean, Missouri, a very small town, the third week of December, 1949.

While Bud is in Olean, Dene feels hard pains that she knows will bring her second child very soon. She has to get to the hospital. It is Saturday, and Bud can't get home until Monday, so Dene calls her parents. She leaves Esther with the landlady until the Pattersons can come pick the little girl up. Dene takes a bus for the short ride to General Hospital as a light snow is falling. She is glad that she has finished wrapping her Christmas gifts. The snow makes getting inside the big heavy door of the hospital almost impossible, as she is in pain. The hospital does not require money ahead of time, which is a relief. The hospital and doctor together charge only $50.00 at

General Hospital. Bud receives a phone call from the Pattersons the evening the baby is born.

"Hello," Mr. Patterson says, "You and Dene have just made us grandparents again."

"Oh no," Bud says, "I wanted to be there with her when the baby came. Is it a girl or boy?"

"It is a healthy boy. Do you have a name picked out?" Mr. Patterson asks.

"Yes," Bud says, "The boy's name is Virgil Lee, named after Mr. Virgil Bower and with my middle name. Is Dene alright?"

"Yes, she's doing fine," Mr. Patterson answers. "She's in room 205. The doctor tells us she will be there only five days. We will keep Esther while Dene is in the hospital. Work is slow now for my wife, and she will love to take time off to take care of Esther at our house."

When Bud arrives in Kansas City by train he goes directly to see Dene and the new baby.

"Hi, you tricky thing; having babies behind my back!" Bud exclaims, by way of announcing his presence as he comes into Dene's hospital room. "How are you two doing?" he asks, kissing her.

"We're both OK, honey," Dene says, smiling. "He weighed seven pounds and 4 ounces and is 21 inches long, just slightly bigger than Esther. You did want to name him Virgil Lee didn't you?"

"Yes," Bud answers. "Will they let me see him?"

"Sure," answers Dene. "He's really cute. He looks just like you."

"You think so?" Bud asks.

"Yes, he doesn't seem to have curly hair, though," she observes. "They won't let me go to the nursery window with you."

Bud asks, "Will you nurse him?"

"I didn't have any luck nursing Esther, so I'm not trying to nurse Virgil. The nurses bring him to me several times a day and let me feed his bottle to him."

"Are they taking good care of you too?"

"Oh, yes. But remember how they wouldn't even let me dangle my feet off the edge of the bed for three days when Esther was born?"

"Yes, they were pretty strict, I remember. They wouldn't let you get up to walk around until close to the end of the week."

"Now they let me sit up awhile each day, and tomorrow I can walk around a little. They say that mothers get their strength back earlier if they move around sooner. I'll be going home in five days."

Bud kisses her again and goes to see baby Virgil through the Nursery window. He is happy to find a healthy-looking baby.

"You did a good job, honey." Bud says when he returns. "He really is cute."

Bud uses a pay phone in the lobby to inform his grandparents about the baby's birth. They are very happy about the new baby. Bud then goes home, getting something to eat on the way.

In 1950, Bud works at the train station in Independence, a town near Kansas City, which also happens to be President Truman's hometown.

One day, the Presidential train comes in. Bud is on the loading platform as President Truman exits the train. The President shakes hands with Bud and asks his name. Bud is thrilled.

Independence is a good place for Bud to work, because it is close enough for him to get home on the train each night. One day while he is working there, Dene takes Esther and Virgil by Greyhound bus to the train depot in Independence. Bud shows them around the station.

When the Missouri Pacific train headed for Kansas City arrives in Independence, Bud takes a picture of Dene and the two children being helped onto the train by the conductor for their *very first train ride.*

At the Kansas City Depot they take a trolley bus back to their apartment.

When Virgil is six months old, Dene begins working at Montgomery Wards Mail Order Department again. Mrs. Perkins has other children, and can't take both Esther and Virgil. Dene goes one block further to a day-care center run by the Salvation Army. They take babies of any age, and care for them through 4 years of age. It is a nice, clean nursery, with several teachers and other workers. They serve breakfast and lunch to the children, for a very low price.

One Friday, Bud is working out of town. Dene does not have the 10 cents she needs for the bus ride to work. She doesn't know what to do. She stands outside the day-care center, trying to figure out who might loan her a dime until that night. One of the workers in the day-care center sees her standing there, away from the bus stop.

She comes out and asks, "Mrs. Weideman, you don't have bus fare for today, do you?"

Dene answers, "No, I don't. I've been trying to figure out how to get to work. I get paid in cash tonight."

The day-care worker says, "Here's 25 cents. You will have bus fare and something to buy lunch with at your cafeteria."

"Oh, thank you," Dene says. "I'll pay you back tonight. How did you know that was my problem?"

The worker answers, "It was obvious because you did not go to the bus stop as usual." They hug, and Dene goes to work.

By July, 1950, Dene finds herself pregnant with a third child. She thinks it would be nice to have two boys close together in age so they can play together.

War clouds come to the United States again, as the Korean War is taking shape. Suddenly, Bud is called back for active duty with the Marines on September 15, 1950. This time he is in the "Air Wing" of the Marines. He is flown to his destinations. He still uses the radio.

Dene takes her children with her on Sundays to a mission church in a store front, which is sponsored by a Baptist Church in the area.

At the end of September, Dene is surprised when both her children come down with a rash. She takes them to the little clinic, where 50 cents pays for a visit to a doctor. He pronounced it Chicken Pox, and sends them home as quickly as possible so they will not expose the other patients. They go home, where Dene uses the landlord's phone to call Montgomery Ward to tell them she will be off work for a few weeks, and to call the Salvation Army Day-Care to tell them she won't be there with the children for awhile. The clinic where Dene took the children sends a nurse to check on them and lets the doctor know how they are progressing. The nurse they send just happens to be a very good girl-friend of Dene's, named Carol. She was a member of their Sunday School Class at Antioch Church.

Virgil is only nine months old, and is getting pretty heavy for Dene to carry up to the third floor. She is anxious for him to start walking. But even then, all those steps will be too much for a toddler to walk every day.

Dene goes to the local health clinic for examinations during her pregnancy. She soon shows signs that she might lose the baby if she doesn't get off her feet more.

Dene and her parents, with Bud's blessing, set out to get Bud discharged so he could help Dene with this problem. They have a lot of red tape to cut through.

On December 18, they celebrate Virgil's first birthday.

That Christmas a Salvation Army bell ringer receives $2.00 from a grateful Dene, who remembers a generous worker's 25 cent gift to her when she was in need.

In February, 1951 Corporal Warren L. (Bud) Weideman is dismissed from duty and out of the reserves on a Hardship Discharge. It is an Honorable Discharge as well. He goes back to work on the Missouri Pacific Railroad.

Robert Warren is born in March, 1951. He turns out to be a healthy baby after all. Bud is working out of town when Dene goes to the hospital, but he gets back just before the baby is born.

This time, General Hospital has what they call "rooming in" as a choice for mothers, so the baby and mother can bond earlier. Dene keeps the baby in her room in a small, movable bed, and can feed and change him. The nursery workers bring the bottles he needs at the correct time. Dene likes it.

Robert has curly hair like Bud's when he is first born. The hospital keeps the mother and baby only three days this time. The ideas about babies are changing rapidly from the time Esther was born, less than three and a half years earlier.

With Bud home and working for the railroad, Dene does not have to work. He travels to far away towns up to 250 miles away, between Kansas City and St. Louis, wherever other station agents need time off for a weekend or a vacation. As a child, Bud wanted to see more of Missouri, and take more train rides. His wish is really coming true.

About the time that Bud is discharged from the reserves, Ralph and Louise move to an apartment in the eastern section of Kansas City. Ralph starts working for TWA in the repair shop. He is in the department that puts words and logos on the plane instruments. It is handy for Ralph, Louise, Bud and Dene to get together on weekends to play cards, alternating apartments each week. They arrive by trolley bus, eat together, put the children to bed, and then the fun begins. They play Canasta or Rummy. The girls play against the guys. The girls think the guys somehow signal each other, because they nearly always beat them. These are fun times, but don't last long because of job situations.

Ralph and Louise move to Gladstone, north of North Kansas City, to be closer to the airport where he works. Bud is able to bid and be accepted for a position as nighttime station agent at the town of Washington, Missouri, about 200 miles from Kansas City.

Bud is unable to find a rental house in Washington, so the hotel owner across the street from the Missouri Pacific Depot tells him, "I have a vacant house about seven miles away in Union, Missouri, and will rent it to you for $50.00 a month."

Bud rents a U-Haul truck, puts their few pieces of furniture, clothes, and kitchenware inside, and drives to Union, and then returns to Kansas City by train. Bud, Dene and the three small children, ages three and a half years, fifteen months, and three months, all take the train to Washington. They are met by their landlord, who takes them to Union.

Dene and Bud are thrilled to rent a little white house on a creek bank.

It has a kitchen, living room, bedroom, bathroom and an upstairs bedroom that is fairly large. There is a small basement. They have a used wringer-type washing machine, and clothes dryer. Dene is thrilled to have their own kitchen sink and their own bathroom, and a large yard for the children to play in.

They have to watch the children carefully to keep them from falling into the creek. It is a fast-running creek when heavy rains come, but most of the time it has only a little water in it. Bud has visions of teaching his sons to catch crawdads and go with them to the near-by Bourbeuse River to fish.

Bud doesn't have a car, so he hitch-hikes to work at the Washington depot, seven miles away. Often, a lady who has a paper route picks him up and gives him a ride. She is going to Washington to pick up her St. Louis Post Dispatch newspapers to distribute about the time Bud is going to work his night shift as station agent. He carries a black lunch bucket, indicating that he is a working man. When Bud comes home in the mornings, the Union family doctor is on his way home from St. Francis Hospital in Washington, where he has already made his patient rounds. He picks Bud up every time he sees him. Sometimes other people pick him up, but mostly it is these two people. Many times he walks all the way there and back.

When the weather starts turning cold, Bud goes to the United Bank of Union and asked for a $100.00 loan to purchase a used car.

The bank teller just says, "How do you want it, cash or check?"

"I'll take the cash, please. Is there something to sign?"

"No," says the teller. Bud has been putting his checks in the bank and writing checks from it, so the bank trusts him to pay the $100.00 without a note.

CHAPTER 10

Life in Union, Missouri and Lake of the Ozarks

In August of 1953 another daughter is born to Bud and Dene. They name her Diana Lynn. She is very cute and has blue eyes like both of her parents, but her hair is brown like her mother's. The doctor who delivers Diana is the same doctor who picked Bud up when he was hitch-hiking to work.

Dene's mother no longer works. Mr. Patterson brings her down to stay with the family while Dene is in the hospital having baby Diana. Dene is in the hospital three days with Diana.

Mrs. Patterson has her hands full, fixing meals for the family and doing the laundry for the two weeks she is there. Somehow, she still manages to make a batch of her famous raised glazed donuts. When the two week visit is over, Mr. Patterson comes back to pick her up.

In September of 1953, Esther starts first grade at the Union Elementary School. The first day, Dene walks her to school. After that she walks with neighborhood children.

At home, the children learn to play quietly, because daddy has to sleep during the daytime so he can go to work at night.

Later that month Dene walks with her children, pushing baby Diana in her stroller, up the hill three blocks to the First Baptist Church. She becomes a member there that first day. Some Sundays Bud is able to go to church with his young family.

Shortly after though, he starts working a second job on weekends. He had previous experience of frying hamburgers, so he applies and is hired by the White Rose Café on Main Street in Union, to be their weekend, daytime fry cook. This extra income helps a lot. They need furniture for their bare house. They buy a used refrigerator, their very first "luxury", plus a gas range for the kitchen. There are a few built-in cupboards. The house is heated by an oil circulating heater in the living/dining room. A round table with legs fashioned like animal paws serves as a place to eat, and for the children to do homework as they begin school. Bud goes to auctions and picks up some additional furniture items that way.

In 1954, Union School District starts their first kindergarten class. Virgil Lee is eligible to attend. The school is seven blocks away from their house, across some very busy streets. The school recommends that kindergartners be brought in a car or bus, and be picked up. Bud's car is parked by their house through the day while he was sleeping. If Dene knew how to drive, she could use it to take Virgil and Esther to school, and then pick up Virgil at noon. A neighbor, who is a pastor of the Christian Church, also has a son who will start kindergarten that September. He introduces himself to Bud and Dene. He offers to teach Dene to drive so she can use the car and take turns with him driving the children to school, and picking the boys up at noon. That seemed like a good deal. Dene learns how to drive the car, and gets her license, even though she has to take the driving test a second time, since she missed a stop sign just before parking at the end of the first test.

During 1955, Bud becomes extremely involved in activities of the community of Union. On Monday, he attends Khoury League meetings. They plan the baseball season for boys in the community, organizing teams with leaders, and finding sponsors for the teams. Bud is voted President of the League in 1955. He organizes a parade led by the high school band, to advertise the fact that these baseball games are free for the public to watch and cheer the players on. When the Weideman boys are old enough, they both play Khoury League baseball. Bud and Dene watch their games. Bud sometimes referees. On Thursdays, Bud bowls with the American Legion team. They bowl in tournaments in various cities. Sometimes Bud is high bowler for his team. One year their team takes third place in a state-wide tournament. Kansas City takes first place, Sedalia second place, and Union third.

Dene begins teaching the Sunday school class of girls that Esther is in. It included girls in grades one through three. That was fun for Dene.

In 1956 Bud attends a Law Enforcement Officers Training School given by the sheriff of the county, with the cooperation of the Federal Bureau of Investigation. After that, he quits working at White Rose Café on weekends, and starts working part time on the Union Police Force. He is paid $1.25 an hour.

Dene's brother Eldon has graduated from college and marries his sweetheart, Patty. Dene and the children go to Kansas City by train to attend the wedding. The

Pattersons pick them up and let them stay at their house to attend the wedding. It is a beautiful wedding. Bud has to stay home and work.

The year of 1957 becomes a big year for Bud and Dene. Bud assists the police chief in teaching a Civil Defense course in first aid to 24 Auxiliary Policemen, who are organized primarily for civil defense, but could be called on for an emergency or disaster.

Bud and Dene are able to purchase their first home. It consists of two stories, containing seven large rooms with high ceilings, and a basement that holds a fuel-oil furnace as well as a front-loading washing machine and a newer dryer. This house purchase is accomplished by another of the programs offered to veterans. They are allowed to buy their first house and pay just 4% interest, with the loan backed by the United States Government. Of course, there is a $200.00 down payment necessary. They obtain a loan of $200.00 from a man Bud had worked with at the White Rose Café.

They also buy their first brand new automobile, a 1957 Chevy. Bud is no longer Agent at the Washington Depot. He has taken a day-time position as Agent at Pacific, Missouri, just fifteen miles from Union.

It is a good thing the family is in the big house, because there is a special need for the extra room on the first floor. They call it "the music room" because they have a used piano there. It has to be turned into a bedroom for Robert, nick-named Bob, who becomes very sick.

Bob and Esther both have their tonsils removed at the hospital in Washington. Esther recovers well, but Bob contracts rheumatic fever. He is not allowed to get off of his back unless someone helps him turn onto his side. Sometimes, he is carried into the living room to lie on the couch, where he can be with the family as they watch television.

It is three months before he is allowed to lean up on his elbow. All this time, the doctor comes to the house once a week to give him a shot of penicillin. The idea is to keep him from getting heart trouble. He has to have someone with him at all times. Dene is there except for when Bud is able to stay with him.

It is difficult for a six-year old. His sister, Diana, plays games with him while he is turned on his side. When he gets well enough to sit up awhile each day, he uses boxes, scissors and crayons to make a doll house and furniture for Diana to play with. A special treat for Bob is the chance to be pulled in his and Virgil's red wagon to the doctor's office instead of the doctor coming to the house. It takes a year for Bob to get well enough to go back to school. Since he had gone only one month to first grade, the school lets him start the next year as though he had never started first grade. By the time he is in fourth grade, he is strong enough to carry his trombone into the school when his mother drives him.

After Bob gets well, Dene thinks she should help out with expenses. She gets a job as waitress at the Union Café. She rather enjoys it, seeing some people she knows, and others she would have no other opportunity to meet otherwise. After about a year she takes a job as a clerk in the Union Variety Store, similar to a Ben Franklin dime store.

Besides being a Sunday school teacher, Dene becomes a leader for a girl's missionary program, where girls learn scriptures, and other things about missions. They go on small, local mission trips to the rest home, hospital and shut-ins. Esther is in the group of mission study girls. Dene also teaches boys and girls in 5th and 6th grades in Sunday school, instead of grades 1 through 3.

Bud gets "bumped" off of his steady job as agent at Pacific by someone with more seniority. But he is able to bump someone else at Eureka, about 30 minutes from Union.

When he gets bumped from Eureka, Bud works on the "extra board", going to whatever city between Kansas City and St. Louis that needs an agent for a day, a week, or extended time. There isn't a single station between St. Louis and Kansas City where he does not work during the years he and his family live in Union, Missouri. This is hectic at times. One schedule finds him in Sedalia every Wednesday, and stations near St. Louis other days or nights of the week. He has to drive to these places because train schedules don't always give him transportation at the times he needs to go.

In March of 1960, a third daughter is born to Bud and Dene at the hospital in Washington, now named St. John's Mercy Hospital.

The baby is named Nancy Jeanne. She has curly blond hair like her daddy had when he was born.

In 1963, Bud is elected Police Judge for the city of Union traffic court. Policemen come to him any time of night necessary to get a warrant for someone's arrest. Anyone "peeling rubber" on city streets might have to clean it up with a tooth brush.

The Weideman children are all in band, and are good students. Virgil is a "crossing guard" when he is in sixth grade. He plays the Coronet in band. Esther and Diana play clarinets. Esther receives a prized John Phillip Sousa Award for excellence on the clarinet her senior year. Nancy plays the flute. She becomes one of the baton twirlers for the high school's marching band. Bob's trombone appears big beside his frail body when he first learns to play it in grade school. Once he is well, however, he plays sports and builds himself up physically. Virgil and Bob are both on the high school basketball teams.

When the children are growing up, Bud and Dene take one week of vacation to go to Kansas City to visit his grandparents, her parents, and her siblings and their families. Bud wants to have the car when they get there, so he takes either the boys or the girls in the car, and Dene takes the other group on the train. Bud always tries to beat the train to each station along the way, and in Jefferson City they stop to eat ice cream at the Howard Johnson's restaurant while they wait for the train. Of course, they buy something for the other children, too. On the return trip, the children switch places.

DENE BECOMES CHURCH SECRETARY

Dene is asked by the pastor of the First Baptist Church if she would consider becoming the church secretary. She studied for that kind of job while in high school and has experience as a typist, so she says yes. Dene becomes secretary to the pastor, and to the church as a whole. She is in charge of keeping financial records and making reports to the church on a monthly basis. The Sunday bulletin and a weekly newsletter mailed to all the members are her responsibility. She also does the correspondence for the pastor, keeps church and Sunday School records, and numerous other things. She enjoys this job and feels she is doing what the Lord wants her to do. After all, in college she felt she was given a call to train up a very good Christian family. This job seems to be right in line with her call. Dene also becomes the Sunday school teacher for a class of married ladies her own age, rather than teaching children.

THE WEIDEMAN CHILDREN GO TO COLLEGE

Bud and Dene's children go to college, soon graduate, and get married. Esther graduates with a degree in English from Central Missouri State College, and later continues her education earning a master's degree in Computer Resources and Information Management from Webster University in Kansas City. Virgil continues his education after marriage and receives a master's degree, and then a Doctorate in Business Administration from Webster University in St. Louis. Bob graduates from Central Missouri State College in Warrensburg, Mo. Diana and Nancy both attend two years of college at the new local East Central Junior College in Union.

EMERGENCY RADIO COMMUNICATIONS

In 1967 Bud becomes station agent at Kirkwood, Missouri for a few years. This is his last station as Agent. It is the largest station between St. Louis and Kansas City, forty-five minutes away from Union, in St. Louis County.

While Bud is working at Kirkwood during the fall of 1968, Missouri Pacific Communications Engineers of St. Louis decide that their telegraphers could use their expertise in code or voice to communicate and help in emergencies such as hurricanes. This could help the railroad as well as the people in the affected areas. Bud buys an amateur (ham) radio and takes the Federal Communications Commission license test so he can join the radio organization that is forming in his company. He is one of the 19 that form the group. They talk on a certain frequency at 9:00 every Sunday morning for a half hour, and again at 4:00 p.m. They train in emergency communications, and learned to be weather spotters with training from the National Weather Bureau.

HAM RADIO OPERATOR

Bud also buys a ham radio for his car. He wants to be able to communicate with Dene if he gets held up in traffic jams, or if she needs to tell him something on his hour's drive home. That means that Dene has to learn Morse code and be able to transmit and receive messages at a rate of 5 words a minute. She must also pass a written test about electronics.   She passes and is granted an amateur radio license. Dene and Bud both upgrade their licenses after about a year. She has to learn to copy 15 words a minute, which is very hard for her. Bud already took over 30 words a minute at his work and in the Marines. He is able to go two steps ahead of Dene.

Dene goes with Bud to yearly training given by the National Weather Bureau for people to become weather spotters.

During these years, Bud joins a Ham Radio club in St. Louis along with some other Missouri Pacific workers that became hams.   He and Dene go to club meetings, and annual "Field Day", where some members spend all weekend in a park, setting up battery-powered radios, and contacting other hams any place in the world that are doing the same thing. Bud and Dene usually stay through Saturday evening, and then go home.

Another fun thing the club members do is have occasional "bunny hunts." This is a chance to use their car radios on direct frequencies (line of sight), without using the club "repeater" that sends signals a long distance.   They have one person giving out signals and some "hints" as to where they were located in their car. The ham radio operator that finds the location first wins the bunny hunt. After they all find the "bunny", they go to a nearby restaurant to eat together.

Bud also joins the Washington, Missouri, ham radio club.   Every year, he and Dene go to their "Hamfest", where ham radio operators and radio equipment stores display items for sale. The hams hope to sell some of their goods, and purchase other equipment.

Once a year, the Kansas City Radio Club also has a big "Hamfest" in the Municipal Auditorium. Bud, Dene, and Esther, and sometimes Bob, go to the Kansas City Hamfest, because Esther and Bob are also hams.   Nancy goes too.   They meet Dene's sister, Louise and Ralph there. Ralph is a ham also. After the Hamfest closes, they eat together at a restaurant before going home.

THE LAKE OF THE OZARKS

Bud works with a man named Larry who owns a mobile home at the Lake of the Ozarks, in central Missouri. Bud thinks he would like to have a place at the Lake of the Ozarks himself. Larry knows of a mobile home near his that is for sale. Larry and his wife go to the lake, with Bud and Dene following them in their car. The mobile home for sale is on what is known as a "second tier" lake lot. The lake is visible, but there is a small road, about one hundred and fifty yards long, between the mobile home and the lakefront. The Weidemans like it.

Bud knows a business man whom he thinks will loan him the money to buy the property. He is right. They are good friends, and the deal is made. It has been a long time since Bud has been fishing. He and Dene think they can go to the lake on weekends and vacations, and eventually spend more time there after retirement. Bud buys a golf cart to drive between the cabin and the lake.

On Bud's way home from work, he notices an old, rather nice looking boat parked beside a home. He stops one day to ask the owner if he wants to sell the boat.

"Yes." the man says, "We don't plan to use it any more. It needs a new motor, but you can have the trailer it's on if you buy the boat. I am asking $500.00." Bud thinks that it is a bargain. He buys the boat, and uses the hitch on his car to bring it home. Dene helps him clean it up. Bud buys a motor. They are set for fun and fishing at the Lake of the Ozarks.

The children and their spouses help Bud and Dene build a large screened-in porch across the front of the mobile home at the lake.

Besides their motor boat, Bud and Dene buy a row boat for fishing. Bud teaches Dene how to row, but Bud rows most of the time. Some of the adult children have fun rowing that boat, while going fishing.

Soon Bud and Dene buy a second, smaller mobile home for their children and their spouses and grand children to use.

Now that they have the lake cabin, Bud and Dene encourage the children to visit them often. They do the same for the relatives from Kansas City. Bud buys a nice ski boat, with a top that can be used when cool days come, and sells the other boat.

Now their vacations and many weekends are spent at the lake. There is grass to cut on the third of an acre they own, and plenty of leaves to rake up and burn in the fall. But it is all fun. It is a delightful place to be. Dene enjoys the chance to decorate the inside of the mobile home, replacing the darker colors she doesn't like with light blue and white paint and wall paper.

After Bud and Dene get their mobile home at the lake set up so they can go at least once a month for a week-end, they also join a radio club at the lake. The club has weekly dinner get-togethers at various restaurants in the area, and an annual picnic which is a lot of fun.

MOVE TO RANCH STYLE HOUSE WITH "RADIO ROOM"

Bud and Dene don't need the two story house in Union, after four of their children are married. They sell it and buy a ranch home that had a "breezeway" between the house and the attached garage. They panel the breezeway and make it into their "Radio Room", with several ham radios, connected to various big antennas out on the back lawn.

RETIREMENT

Bud and Dene both retire on the same date, September 15, 1986. Bud worked for Missouri Pacific, now known as Union Pacific, for 38 years. Dene worked as church secretary for 22 years. Each company gives them retirement parties. Then the family gives them a retirement party. It is a Hawaiian-themed party, because Bud and Dene talked about wanting to go to Hawaii after retirement. They change their minds, however, and go to Florida instead. They visit Dene's brother Eldon and his wife Patty in Coral Springs, Florida. They take Bud and Dene to a Hawaiian dinner theater restaurant. They also go to Pompano Beach, where they swim in the ocean. This is the first time Dene has ever seen the ocean. They enjoy the ocean, but decide not to go fishing at the ocean. They prefer fishing at the lake.

Retirement gives them a chance to spend about three weeks each month at the lake from spring through fall. Dene goes to a church near their "cabin", as they call it. They go home to Union at the end of the month to pay the bills. These days at the lake become treasured times.

By this time all of the Weideman children are married and grandchildren are born and growing up.

Bud and Dene buy a third boat. It is a deck boat, with a flat-surface deck and flat canvas top. Dene steers the boat some. Mostly, Bud is captain, except when one of the grandchildren is sitting on his lap, "steering" the boat, and wearing his captain's hat. This is the boat they have when they retire.

Bud teaches Dene how to bait her hook and clean the fish she catches. One time she casts a baited rod and hits her head with the hook. That takes them on an emergency trip to the doctor's office for a tetanus shot.

Their grandchildren love the smell of grandma's big breakfasts as they awake at the lake. There is bacon or sausage with eggs, and waffles or pancakes. Other times it is hash browns with eggs, sausage and biscuits.

They love swinging on a swing made from a rubber tire, which Grandma paints to look like a horse. They name him "Old Champ." The grandchildren catch tadpoles, as well as tiny frogs, lightning bugs, and cocoons they keep in a jar with holes in the lid. Each day they watch to see the metamorphosis into butterflies.

Something that keeps Dene busy is making quilts. She makes "theme" quilts for all of the children and grandchildren, as well as making a "train" quilt for Bud, and a "diamond" quilt to use as a spread for their bed in Union.

DID BUD CATCH THE BIG FISH?

Evenings at the lake are wonderful, sitting on the screened-in porch watching boats on the water as well as near-by campers coming and going. It is a "family-like" atmosphere where they get to know everyone around, and often have visitors and dinners together by the lake.

Bud tells Dene one evening, "I used to think that catching a "big fish" was really important."

"I know," she says.

He continues, "Now I think I have caught the best "fish" in the world!"

"What do you mean?" she inquires.

"I was lucky enough to "catch" you—the sweetest girl in the world, my little "five-foot two girl with eyes of blue", as the song goes. I think that is a tremendous feat for a poor "fisher boy" that lived down by the river."

"That is very touching, Bud. But I think I'm the lucky one. You are smart, good looking, and very good at every thing you do. You are a strong person who has taught our children the value of hard work, getting their education, and living by truths from the Bible. Not only that, but you are a hero from two wars."

They sit swinging on the porch, which reminds them of the early days of their youth when they sat on the Pattersons' front porch swing, looking towards the future.

Dene says, after a few kisses and hugs, "I really believe God led us together, and kept you safe to help me fulfill his mission for me, raising a very good Christian family."

GOLDEN WEDDING ANNIVERSARY CELEBRATION

As time passes, Bud and Dene celebrate their golden wedding anniversary. Their children give them two parties at the Lake of the Ozarks. The first one is in a rented hall, where slides of their life together are shown to family and friends after a buffet lunch, punch and anniversary cake.

The second party, later that evening, is held under a pavilion near the lake, close to their cabin. Everyone helps themselves to a picnic dinner provided by their children. Then some men from the neighborhood play country music. Bud and Dene haven't danced together since early days in Union when Bud turned on country music on the radio and lead Dene to the kitchen, where there was linoleum flooring. They danced, and sometimes sang the songs to each other. On this special night of their 50th wedding anniversary celebration, Bed and Dene dance together, dance after dance.

CHOOSE ONE – LAKE OF THE OZARKS OR UNION

Gradually, Bud and Dene realize that they need to live in one house or the other. They are getting too old to keep up two places. So, they pray together about it. They put the house in Union up for sale. They pray that if the house does not sell by a certain time, then they will know that it is meant for them to sell the lake house. The Lord answers by not letting the house in Union sell in the specified time. So they sell the lake property and return to their home in Union full time.

60TH WEDDING ANNIVERSARY AND 81ST BIRTHDAY

In August of 2006, Bud and Dene celebrate their 60th wedding anniversary in Union with their children, grandchildren and great grandchildren around them.

Bud has had some health problems the doctors have worked on for several years. He is in the hospital the first week of September. His 81st birthday is coming up September 14th. While Bud is in the hospital, a heart specialist is called in. He runs many tests. Based on the test results, the heart specialist tells Dene to call all the children to the hospital so he can talk to them. All the children come to Bud's hospital room the next morning, where Dene has been staying over night with him, sleeping in the extra bed in the room. They all listen as the doctor tells them that three of Bud's vital organs are shutting down. He says Bud has only a few weeks to live.

The hospital arranges for Bud to go home and have Hospice workers go to the house daily to see how Bud is doing, and report to the doctor. He needs oxygen to help his breathing. Bud has been a smoker since he was in the Marines. He knows that he can't smoke with oxygen tanks in the house.

Dene has never smoked, but on the way home from the hospital, Bud shows his teasing nature is still alive and well.

He says to Dene, "Now Dene, you know that you can't smoke any more."

"Oh darn, that's too bad," she mutters.

The family gathers at the house to celebrate Bud's 81st birthday on the 14th of September.   There are the five children and their spouses, 10 grandchildren, and 8 great-grandchildren. One great-great grandchild could not be there.   Bob's wife, Deb, and one of his daughters, Carla, play many hymns for Bud after the dinner.

Bud says, "This is the happiest birthday of my life."

LIFE ON EARTH ENDS

Bud speaks to each of his children individually to ask them to forgive him for anything they might have held against him in his life.   He also says that to Dene.   They have nothing held against him, and tell him so.

The next two weeks Dene stays by Bud's side and has one of their children with her most of the time. The children prepare a CD of Bud's favorite hymns, so they can be played in the bedroom all day long.   Also, there are pictures of the family shown over and over on a computer screen placed where Bud can see them.

A minister, whom Bud asks for, comes by.   He talks to Bud about what it was like to be a Marine.   Bud tells him he prayed a lot, and read the Bible often while he was in the Marines.   There were long trips on the troop ships where he could spend time reading. Bud asks the minister to pray for him.

Dene speaks.   She says, "Honey, you've been asking each of us to forgive you for sins.   Now you can ask Jesus to forgive your sins and his blood will pour down over your head and wash you white as snow."

"Look at that," Bud says, smiling.   "I've had a preacher in the house all the time."

The minister then asks Bud to pray out loud with him. Bud does just that, asking for forgiveness for all his sins. Bud tells the minister that he feels really blessed to have family, hospice workers and other friends to take care of him. He says he is concerned about poor old men out on the streets, sick and dying with nobody to care for them.

After the minister leaves, Bud has a private conversation with Dene. He says, "I want to see Jesus."

Dene says, "You know, honey, we want to live forever, but we don't want to live in old beat-up bodies like we get here on earth. It's like flowers that die and their seeds fall to the ground and new flowers spring up."

Bud interrupts, "So when you see flowers blooming in the spring, you will know I am 'blooming' in heaven."

"Yes, I will remember."

After a pause of contemplation Bud says, "I want to see the face of Jesus."

Dene says, "Soon Jesus will send his angels to come and get you and take you to Heaven to be with Jesus." She pauses, holding back tears, then says, "When the time comes, we will miss you very, very much, but it's O.K. to go. We will be alright. Going to Heaven is what we all want to do eventually. You just get to go first."

Bud smiles his familiar, twinkling blue-eyed smile, and goes to sleep.

The next morning he leaves to go be with Jesus. Dene knows for sure that Fisher Boy was the biggest, best fisher of all. She remembers that Jesus used fishermen to fish for men to become followers of Jesus. Surely Fisher Boy's life will help keep his children and grandchildren working for Jesus all their lives.

Bud is buried with full military honors at Jefferson Barracks National Cemetery in St. Louis, Missouri.

Dene tells everyone, "While I am grieving my loss of Bud, I am, at the same time, thrilled to know for sure that he is in Heaven with Jesus. That is what Bud wanted when he knew it was time to leave this earth. The Lord has blessed us together all these years. I know one day Fisher Boy and I will meet again in Heaven, and all our children and grandchildren will meet there too, since they have given their hearts to Jesus also."

Praise the Lord God Almighty!! Amen and Amen.

Postscript

Since Bud left this earth I have been surrounded with God's love, through our family and my pastor and the other members of my church family. I am proud to share my testimony of my experience when I became a Christian.

> A dream three nights in a row started my new life with Jesus.
>
> There it was, a banner unfurled across the sky, with all the names of saved people on it! I looked, but my name was not there. The same thing happened two more nights. I awoke. I felt devastated, yet I understood. The Holy Spirit was talking to me, telling me Jesus wanted to save me. Then my name would be written in Heaven.
>
> So I talked quietly to Jesus.
> "I'm no good." (Even an 11 year old like me had been rebellious to my parents at times.)
> "But if you want me, you can have me. Please forgive my sins and come into my heart. I will live for you the rest of my life."
> I felt peaceful. I know Jesus saved me right then. I felt like a new person, and I was.

I hope my testimony will help others to recognize when the Holy Spirit is talking to them, telling them that Jesus wants to save them, so that their names will be written in Heaven.

Who is Fisher Boy?

Born with polio, cured with the help of a Navaho squaw's remedies, Fisher Boy's life takes intriguing and surprising turns, including escapes from a house fire, a devastating flood, a raging river whirlpool, and the loss of his parents, all before his 21st birthday.

Fisher Boy, also known as Buddy and Bud, overcomes all the odds, catching a big fish to be proud of, achieving an Eagle Scout award, serving proudly as a US Marine, and marrying Dene, his high school sweetheart and soul mate, the author of this book.

About the Author

Dene and Bud met in High School, married when he returned from the war, and raised a wonderful family of five children. Their lives together, spanning 60 years, and her knowledge of Bud's life as a child, highly qualify Dene to tell his story.

Shortly before Bud died, he told Dene about an idea he had for a book. He said it would be about a Fisher Boy. The question would be: "Did Fisher Boy catch the biggest fish, or did he catch a girl?" Bud said he would dictate the story to Dene; however his life on earth was at an end. Dene decided to write the story for Bud, based on his life.